RIBA Plan of Work 2013 Guide
Town Planning

The RIBA Plan of Work 2013 Guides

Other titles in the series:

Design Management, by Dale Sinclair
Project Leadership, by Nick Willars
Contract Administration, by Ian Davies

Coming in 2015:

Information Exchanges
Sustainability
Conservation
Health and Safety
Handover Strategy

The RIBA Plan of Work 2013 is endorsed by the following organisations:

Royal Incorporation of
Architects in Scotland

CIAT
Chartered Institute of
Architectural Technologists

Royal Society of
Architects in Wales

Construction
Industry Council

Royal Society
of Ulster Architects

RIBA Plan of Work 2013 Guide

Town Planning

Ruth Reed

RIBA **Publishing**

© RIBA Enterprises Ltd, 2014
Published by RIBA Publishing, The Old Post Office, St Nicholas Street,
Newcastle upon Tyne NE1 1RH

ISBN 978 1 85946 553 0
Stock code 82653

British Library Cataloguing in Publication Data
A catalogue record for this book is available from the British Library.

Commissioning Editor: Sarah Busby
Series Editor: Dale Sinclair
Project Manager: Alasdair Deas
Design: Kneath Associates
Typesetting: Academic+Technical, Bristol, UK
Printed and bound by CPI Group (UK) Ltd
Cover image: © iStock/Studio Three Dots

Picture credits
Page 106: Crown Copyright

RIBA Publishing is part of RIBA Enterprises Ltd
www.ribaenterprises.com

Contents

Foreword

Understanding the planning system and its processes is essential for anyone engaged in development and obtaining the relevant planning consents are key components of successful project delivery.

The National Planning Policy Framework is a key part of the government's reforms to make the planning system less complex and more accessible. The framework sets out the government's policy for decision-takers, both in drawing up plans and making decisions about planning applications, and has been the cornerstone in progressive reform of the planning process.

This guide usefully charts the planning processes against the stages of the RIBA Plan of Work 2013, setting out the routes to achieving consent for development and the strategies that can be adopted, and their implications for project timescales and budgets.

It is clear that early consultation with the planning authority and key stakeholders for the development project contributes to a successful outcome.

The greater the understanding of how to successfully align the development process with planning, the better the planning system can be in responding to the demands put upon it.

Steve Quartermain
Chief Planner
Department for Communities and Local Government

Series editor's foreword

The RIBA Plan of Work 2013 was developed in response to the needs of an industry adjusting to emerging digital design processes, disruptive technologies and new procurement models, as well as other drivers. A core challenge is to communicate the thinking behind the new RIBA Plan in greater detail. This process is made more complex because the RIBA Plan of Work has existed for 50 years and is embodied within the psyche and working practices of everyone involved in the built environment sector. Its simplicity has allowed it to be interpreted and used in many ways, underpinning the need to explain the content of the Plan's first significant edit. By relating the Plan to a number of commonly encountered topics, the *RIBA Plan of Work 2013 Guides* series forms a core element of the communication strategy and I am delighted to be acting as the series editor.

The first strategic shift in the RIBA Plan of Work 2013 was to acknowledge a change from the tasks of the design team to those of the project team: the client, design team and contractor. Stages 0 and 7 are part of this shift, acknowledging that buildings are used by clients, or their clients, and, more importantly, recognising the paradigm shift from designing for construction towards the use of high-quality design information to help facilitate better whole-life outcomes.

New procurement strategies focused around assembling the right project team are the beginnings of significant adjustments in the way that buildings will be briefed, designed, constructed, operated and used. Design teams are harnessing new digital design technologies (commonly bundled under the BIM wrapper), linking geometric information to new engineering analysis software to create a generation of buildings that would not previously have been possible. At the same time, coordination processes and environmental credentials are being improved. A core focus is the progressive fixity of high-quality information – for the first time, the right information at the right time, clearly defining who does what, when.

The RIBA Plan of Work 2013 aims to raise the knowledge bar on many subjects, including sustainability, Information Exchanges and health and safety. The *RIBA Plan of Work 2013 Guides* are crucial tools in disseminating and explaining how these themes are fully addressed and how the new Plan can be harnessed to achieve the new goals and objectives of our clients.

Dale Sinclair
November 2014

Acknowledgements and dedication

Thanks are due to:

Ian Leighton for proofreading, sanity checks and cups of tea.

The directors and staff of Green Planning Studio for real-world commentary and advice especially:

Matthew Green
Michael Rudd
Joe Salt
Eleanor Kidd
Charlotte Greenway

All those involved in the production of the book, in particular:

Sarah Busby, RIBA Publishing
Dale Sinclair
Steve Quartermain
Ann Skippers
Ian Hunter

About the author

Ruth Reed is an architect and academic with a distinguished reputation in planning issues. She has experience as a planning inspector and a lobbyist on planning matters for the RIBA. She is currently a partner at Green Planning Studio Limited, a planning consultancy with an enviable record in winning planning appeals. Ruth previously set up Reed Architects in 1992, where she rapidly won a reputation for gaining planning consents. Much of the practice's work was in the self-build sector and Ruth joined and became a director of Associated Self-Build Architects.

Ruth was elected as the first female president of the RIBA in 2009. As president, her policy focus was on architectural education and on planning reform. Once her term had finished Ruth took over chairmanship of the Planning Group and continues to represent the profession to policymakers in this area. Since the presidency she has served on the RIBA Education Committee and the University of Cambridge Building Committee and is currently a vice-chair of the Construction Industry Council Board. As a previous RIBA council member she has also been Vice President of Membership and chair of the RIBA CPD Subcommittee, where she drafted the introduction of the core curriculum. Ruth has examined at the Welsh School of Architecture and also at Plymouth and Bath Universities. Most recently she was a professor and course director for the Postgraduate Diploma in Architecture Practice at Birmingham School of Architecture.

About the series editor

Dale Sinclair is Director of Technical Practice for AECOM's architecture team in EMEA. He is an architect and was previously a director at Dyer and an associate director at BDP. He has taught at Aberdeen University and the Mackintosh School of Architecture and regularly lectures on BIM, design management and the RIBA Plan of Work 2013. He is passionate about developing new design processes that can harness digital technologies, manage the iterative design process and improve design outcomes.

He is currently the RIBA Vice President, Practice and Profession, a trustee of the RIBA Board, a UK board member of BuildingSMART and a member of various CIC working groups. He was the editor of the *BIM Overlay to the Outline Plan of Work 2007*, edited the RIBA Plan of Work 2013 and was author of its supporting tools and guidance publications: *Guide to Using the RIBA Plan of Work 2013* and *Assembling the Collaborative Project Team*.

Introduction

Overview

This guide charts the planning processes against the stages of the RIBA Plan of Work 2013, setting out the different routes to achieving consent for development and the strategies that can be adopted and their implications for project timescales and budgets.

It provides current information and advice on the policy and process frameworks for planning as both an informative text and also as an aide-memoire. As such it is useful to students of architecture, related built environment professions and any member of a project team.

Context

Town and country planning legislation is different in each of the home nations and the information and advice in this guide applies to the English planning system. England and Wales share the same primary legislation so the strategic level of process is common to both, but guidance and national policy differ and readers should refer to Welsh Government requirements before making applications in Wales.

In March 2012 the Department for Communities and Local Government introduced the National Planning Policy Framework for England (NPPF), which reduced over 1,000 pages of national policy to around 50. It abolished the national Planning Policy Statements and the earlier national Planning Policy Guidance notes and put in place a presumption in favour of sustainable development to stimulate growth and overcome inertia in the production of development plans. The Planning Practice Guidance to support the NPPF, which supersedes many circulars and other guidance, was introduced as updatable online pages in spring 2014. This radical change to the system requires a new approach to developing a planning strategy for a development, which is addressed in this guide.

How to use this book

The guide describes the processes and policies that are essential to obtaining planning consent in the new policy environment. It can be used to develop a successful planning strategy and as a guide to the process. The text contains information, checklists, risk matrices and examples to inform and use as tools. It should be read in conjunction with the *Guide to Using the RIBA Plan of Work 2013*, the *RIBA Job Book* (ninth edition) and the companion guides in this series to put the tasks relating to town planning into context with the other activities at each stage of the RIBA Plan of Work.

Who?

The lead role in the activities at each stage can be undertaken by different members of the project team. For example the initial planning strategy may be part of the advice provided by the client adviser at Stage 0. For straightforward projects and smaller developments the site investigation, pre-application discussions, application, monitoring and discharge of pre-commencement conditions may be undertaken by the architect in Stages 1 to 4. In more complex cases a specialist planning consultant may be appointed to the same stages and be a core member of the design team. This could be where a detailed planning strategy, management of the consultants providing supporting information and complex negotiations and legal agreements and possibly even appeals are required.

When?

An early understanding of the possible constraints arising from the surveys and assessments required to support a planning case can reduce delay in making a valid application. As early as Stage 0, activities such as ecological surveys and financial viability studies can be undertaken to prepare the application and inform both the Strategic Brief and the Initial Project Brief. The outcomes of these investigations may impact on the Business Case for the project, therefore obtaining early information is advisable to avoid abortive work.

Once a planning strategy has been determined it may be deemed advisable to make an early outline application or to apply for certificates of lawfulness. These can be undertaken at Stage 1. A report on the Site Information and planning strategy will inform the Initial Project Brief at Stage 1.

Clients may not wish to incur the costs of a complete design team until planning approval has been obtained. Applying for planning permission on the basis of the Concept Design at Stage 2, however, carries risks due to incomplete Site Information and, later on, problems associated with the coordination of other design team member Information Exchanges with the approved scheme.

Because of the risks associated with the decision-making process it is strongly advised that detailed consent or approval of any reserved matters is applied for at Stage 3 Developed Design and obtained before Stage 4 Technical Design is commenced. In all cases it is unlawful to commence development works (Stage 5 Construction) before consent is obtained and pre-commencement conditions discharged. It should be noted that there may be conditions that are discharged during or after the construction stage that may be the contractual responsibility of the contractor within the Building Contract but remain the legal responsibility of the landowner.

Managing risk in the planning process

The planning process is risky. Those advising the client should avoid making definitive predictions of outcomes as the decision-making system is subject to political vagaries. Timescales in particular are uncertain. Resource problems within local authorities affect their ability to provide a timely service at all stages. Local knowledge is helpful in advising clients about possible delays.

Obtaining planning approval can add significantly to the value of a client's building or land, but set against this is the cost of the application. The likely costs should be factored into the Project Budget from the outset, and can include the costs of surveys, consultant reports, legal advice and representation, planning fees and payment of the Community Infrastructure Levy. The mitigation of harm identified as part of the planning case, whether by installing flood barriers or bat boxes, can be a costly extra if not identified accurately and early in the Project Budget.

Summary

As each application is determined on a case-by-case basis, planning can be a fascinating but frequently frustrating process. Other areas of legislation have a significant impact on planning, particularly environmental law, and the project lead will require a broad knowledge of other disciplines to manage the team of consultants frequently required to put together a valid planning application. Planning provides architects with the opportunity to extend their services to include areas of specialist knowledge, such as the historic environment, landscape, urban design and the planning system itself, necessary to support the applications that they make on behalf of their clients. As the one activity that adds the most identifiable value to a project, the skills and knowledge that lead to successful applications should never be undersold.

The RIBA Plan of Work 2013 provides the framework for identifying the planning tasks that will be undertaken on a project. This assists in identifying and scheduling the fees that may be accrued for this work, as well as the relationships with other activities at each stage.

Ruth Reed
November 2014

Using this series

For ease of reference each book in this series is broken down into chapters that map on to the stages of the Plan of Work. So, for instance, the first chapter covers the tasks and considerations around town planning at Stage 0.

We have also included several in-text features to enhance your understanding of the topic. The following key will explain what each icon means and why each feature is useful to you:

 The 'Example' feature explores an example from practice, either real or theoretical

 The 'Tools and Templates' feature outlines standard tools, letters and forms and how to use them in practice

 The 'Signpost' feature introduces you to further sources of trusted information from books, websites and regulations

 The 'Definition' feature explains key terms in this topic area in more detail

 The 'Hints and Tips' feature dispenses pragmatic advice and highlights common problems and solutions

 The 'Small Project Observation' feature highlights useful variations in approach and outcome for smaller projects

RIBA ⌖

The **RIBA Plan of Work 2013** organises the process of briefing, designing, constructing, maintaining, operating and using building projects into a number of key stages. The content of stages may vary or overlap to suit specific project requirements.

RIBA Plan of Work 2013

Stages ▸ Tasks ▾	**0** Strategic Definition	**1** Preparation and Brief	**2** Concept Design	**3** Developed Design
Core Objectives	Identify client's **Business Case** and **Strategic Brief** and other core project requirements.	Develop **Project Objectives**, including **Quality Objectives** and **Project Outcomes**, **Sustainability Aspirations**, **Project Budget**, other parameters or constraints and develop **Initial Project Brief**. Undertake **Feasibility Studies** and review of **Site Information**.	Prepare **Concept Design**, including outline proposals for structural design, building services systems, outline specifications and preliminary **Cost Information** along with relevant **Project Strategies** in accordance with **Design Programme**. Agree alterations to brief and issue **Final Project Brief**.	Prepare **Developed Design**, including coordinated and updated proposals for structural design, building services systems, outline specifications, **Cost Information** and **Project Strategies** in accordance with **Design Programme**.
Procurement *Variable task bar	Initial considerations for assembling the project team.	Prepare **Project Roles Table** and **Contractual Tree** and continue assembling the project team.	⟵ The procurement strategy does not fundamentally alter the progression of the design or the level of detail prepared at	a given stage. However, **Information Exchanges** will vary depending on the selected procurement route and **Building Contract**. A bespoke **RIBA Plan of Work**
Programme *Variable task bar	Establish **Project Programme**.	Review **Project Programme**.	Review **Project Programme**.	⟵ The procurement route may dictate the **Project Programme** and result in certain stages overlapping
(Town) Planning *Variable task bar	Pre-application discussions.	Pre-application discussions.	⟵ Planning applications are typically made using the Stage 3 output.	A bespoke **RIBA Plan of Work 2013** will identify when the
Suggested Key Support Tasks	Review **Feedback** from previous projects.	Prepare **Handover Strategy** and **Risk Assessments**. Agree **Schedule of Services**, **Design Responsibility Matrix** and **Information Exchanges** and prepare **Project Execution Plan** including **Technology** and **Communication Strategies** and consideration of **Common Standards** to be used.	Prepare **Sustainability Strategy, Maintenance and Operational Strategy** and review **Handover Strategy** and **Risk Assessments**. Undertake third party consultations as required and any **Research and Development** aspects. Review and update **Project Execution Plan**. Consider **Construction Strategy**, including offsite fabrication, and develop **Health and Safety Strategy**.	Review and update **Sustainability, Maintenance and Operational** and **Handover Strategies** and **Risk Assessments**. Undertake third party consultations as required and conclude **Research and Development** aspects. Review and update **Project Execution Plan**, including **Change Control Procedures**. Review and update **Construction** and **Health and Safety Strategies**.
Sustainability Checkpoints	**Sustainability Checkpoint — 0**	**Sustainability Checkpoint — 1**	**Sustainability Checkpoint — 2**	**Sustainability Checkpoint — 3**
Information Exchanges (at stage completion)	**Strategic Brief.**	**Initial Project Brief.**	**Concept Design** including outline structural and building services design, associated **Project Strategies**, preliminary **Cost Information** and **Final Project Brief**.	**Developed Design**, including the coordinated architectural, structural and building services design and updated **Cost Information**.
UK Government Information Exchanges	Not required.	Required.	Required.	Required.

*Variable task bar – in creating a bespoke project or practice specific RIBA Plan of Work 2013 via www.ribaplanofwork.com a specific bar is selected from a number of options.

The **RIBA Plan of Work 2013** should be used solely as guidance for the preparation of detailed professional services contracts and building contracts.

www.ribaplanofwork.com

4 Technical Design	5 Construction	6 Handover and Close Out	7 In Use
Prepare **Technical Design** in accordance with **Design Responsibility Matrix** and **Project Strategies** to include all architectural, structural and building services information, specialist subcontractor design and specifications, in accordance with **Design Programme**.	Offsite manufacturing and onsite **Construction** in accordance with **Construction Programme** and resolution of **Design Queries** from site as they arise.	Handover of building and conclusion of **Building Contract**.	Undertake **In Use** services in accordance with **Schedule of Services**.
2013 will set out the specific tendering and procurement activities that will occur at each stage in relation to the chosen procurement route.	Administration of **Building Contract**, including regular site inspections and review of progress.	Conclude administration of **Building Contract**.	
or being undertaken concurrently. A bespoke **RIBA Plan of Work 2013** will clarify the stage overlaps.	The **Project Programme** will set out the specific stage dates and detailed programme durations.		
planning application is to be made.			
Review and update **Sustainability, Maintenance and Operational** and **Handover Strategies** and **Risk Assessments**. Prepare and submit Building Regulations submission and any other third party submissions requiring consent. Review and update **Project Execution Plan**. Review **Construction Strategy**, including sequencing, and update **Health and Safety Strategy**.	Review and update **Sustainability Strategy** and implement **Handover Strategy**, including agreement of information required for commissioning, training, handover, asset management, future monitoring and maintenance and ongoing compilation of **'As-constructed' Information**. Update **Construction** and **Health and Safety Strategies**.	Carry out activities listed in **Handover Strategy** including **Feedback** for use during the future life of the building or on future projects. Updating of **Project Information** as required.	Conclude activities listed in **Handover Strategy** including **Post-occupancy Evaluation**, review of **Project Performance**, **Project Outcomes** and **Research and Development** aspects. Updating of **Project Information**, as required, in response to ongoing client **Feedback** until the end of the building's life.
Sustainability Checkpoint — 4	**Sustainability Checkpoint — 5**	**Sustainability Checkpoint — 6**	**Sustainability Checkpoint — 7**
Completed **Technical Design** of the project.	**'As-constructed' Information**.	Updated **'As-constructed' Information**.	**'As-constructed' Information** updated in response to ongoing client **Feedback** and maintenance or operational developments.
Not required.	Not required.	Required.	As required.

© RIBA

Planning actions in the RIBA Plan of Work 2013 may include the following tasks:

RIBA Plan of Work 2013

Stages

	0 Strategic Definition	**1** Preparation and Brief	**2** Concept Design	**3** Developed Design
Tasks	0.1 Identify planning requirements in the Strategic Brief	1.1 Assemble planning and Site Information	2.1 Continue pre-application discussions	3.1 Identify the correct form of consent
	0.2 Identify impacts on Project Programme and Initial Project Brief	1.2 Identify planning context	2.2 Use design review	3.2 Prepare drawings and BIM models for planning
	0.3 Devise planning strategy	1.3 Submit application to establish use	2.3 Other consultations	3.3 Prepare other supporting documentation, fees and certificates
		1.4 Identify other relevant legislation	2.4 Community liaison	3.4 Make application based on Stage 3 outputs
		1.5 Conduct pre-application discussions	2.5 Coordinate consultant submissions	3.5 Obtain validation for application
		1.6 Identify validation requirements	2.6 Develop design and access statement	3.6 Support the decision-making process
		1.7 Prepare Stage 1 planning and Site Information report	2.7 Prepare planning statement for Stage 2 report	3.7 Make an appeal
			2.8 Make planning applications based on Stage 2 outputs	

4 **Technical Design**	5 **Construction**	6 **Handover and Close Out**	7 **In Use**
4.1 **Make applications for pre-commencement conditions**	5.1 **Make applications for Construction stage conditions**	6.1 **Comply with pre-occupancy conditions**	7.1 **Comply with in-use conditions**
4.2 **Challenge conditions through application or appeal**	5.2 **Determine responsibility for compliance with conditions during construction**		7.2 **Review implementation of the planning strategy**
4.3 **Apply for material and non-material amendments to the project**	5.3 **Apply for material and non-material amendments to the project**		7.3 **Advise client on planning enforcement**
4.4 **Make applications for listed building consent**	5.4 **Provide planning documentation for 'As-constructed Information'**		

Stage 0

Strategic
Definition

Chapter overview

Stage 0 is new to the RIBA Plan of Work 2013. At this stage a project is strategically appraised and defined before a detailed brief is created. The Core Objectives are to identify the client's Business Case and Strategic Brief. This may require investigation of a number of sites or alternative options, such as extensions, refurbishment or new buildings. Each option will have planning implications that need to be considered. In order to do this the planning context needs to be understood and set out for each option and the implications for the Project Programme and the Project Budget identified.

The key coverage in this chapter is as follows:

Identifying the implications of planning requirements in the Strategic Brief

Understanding the plan-led system

How planning decisions are made:
- material considerations
- harm
- permitted development
- change of use

The planning process – impacts on the Project Programme and Project Budget

Devising a planning strategy

Introduction

Planning considerations are a key component of the strategic appraisal that underpins the client's Business Case for a project. In order to provide accurate advice at this stage, the client's adviser needs to understand the planning implications of the options before them. This chapter describes the policy and process context for planning, how it can affect the potential viability of a proposal and how it can be influenced to meet the long-term strategic aims of the client.

It is important to understand how policies are developed, how they are influenced by government guidance and how, in turn, this affects the weight given to policies by decision makers. An understanding of policy development can enable the client and the client's advisers to influence policymakers before new development plans are adopted; with this knowledge they can put in place long-term strategic proposals and develop master plans for major phased developments.

Also essential is an understanding of the process of obtaining planning approval and the considerable impact this can have on the Project Programme and Project Budget. Each option should be analysed to predict any planning issues. The client may choose an option with fewer potential problems in order to minimise the risk of delay and/or costly mitigation. Alternatively, early negotiations with the planning authority may resolve or minimise any potential conflicts with policy.

This advice can be provided to the client by the architect/project lead or a specialist adviser. The implications of decisions made at Stage 0 are far reaching and essential to the project's success. The planning strategy is a key component of this decision making so the advice needs to be comprehensive and authoritative.

What are the Core Objectives of this stage?

The Core Objectives of the RIBA Plan of Work 2013 at Stage 0 are:

Tasks ▼	**0** Strategic Definition
Core Objectives	Identify client's **Business Case** and **Strategic Brief** and other core project requirements.

The Business Case for the project and the Strategic Brief for its successful delivery will include the planning strategy. This may be developed from the appraisal of a number of sites and planning options or begin as a master plan for a long-term development strategy.

Identifying the implications of planning requirements in the Strategic Brief

The Strategic Brief should set out the broad vision of the client's aims and identify possible routes to achieving the Project Outcomes. It may begin with an analysis of the existing estate, exploring alterations, extension and refurbishment of existing buildings before identifying the Business Case for new buildings and even relocation. Each option has planning implications, and for long-term development strategies actions at Stage 0 may include engagement with policymaking to ensure the principle of development is established ahead of making any applications.

For smaller sites or where the project type and planning environment are well understood, the knowledge and experience of the general architect practitioner is usually sufficient to provide planning advice. For more complex projects or where the potential constraints and planning outcome are uncertain, the specialist advice of a planning consultant is essential.

In order to assess the planning implications for each option, the planning context for each site and proposal needs to be understood. The context will include national and local plan policies that form the development plan and that will be relevant to the decision maker if an application is made. This underpinning principle of a plan-led system is described below.

Also important to the strategic consideration of the development options is the process that may have to be undertaken to achieve planning permission for each. For example, a new-build option may require an outline application to establish the use of the land or buildings, possibly setting out a master plan for future phased development. Any planning application in this scenario will be in two stages: the outline application and the application for reserved matters. This route will take more time, but it is used to reduce the risk of the use of the land being unacceptable to the local planning authority (LPA) and to establish some principles, such as access and layout.

For smaller projects it is equally important to communicate the requirements of the planning process to the client to ensure that their expectations for the Project Programme are tempered by the reality of the system and the attendant risks of delay. For example, even a replacement dwelling can be resisted by the local planning committee because of lobbying from neighbours:

Political delays to a domestic project

The client purchases a bungalow on a large plot on the edge
of a village but within the development boundary. There are no
local plan policies restricting the size of replacement dwellings
and the new house will not be visible from any public viewpoint.
However, one local resident who will be able to see the new
dwelling makes strong objections to the local councillors, who
decide that the application should go to committee rather than
have it decided under delegated powers. The officers, who
have supported the application, delay the decision. The client
is advised to obtain a refusal and appeal rather than appeal for
non-determination without knowledge of the council's case. The
Project Programme is delayed by six months, creating additional
mortgage costs for the client and a great deal of frustration.

Understanding the plan-led system

The planning system in England has been an exemplar to other countries,
with its underpinning principle of a plan-led system. Decision makers –
whether they are local authority planning officers under delegated powers,
the planning committee, inspectors appointed by the Secretary of State or
the Secretary of State in person – decide whether consent should be given
based on the development plan policies that apply to the development
proposal and the weight that may be given to them. The development plan
policies are bespoke to each LPA and are developed through a process
of public consultation and examination by the Planning Inspectorate. As
this determines what development is likely to be granted consent in the
future, architects should engage in the plan-making process by acting as
consultees to ensure that the values of good sustainable design and their
clients' objectives are reflected in the approved plan.

Development plan

The development plan consists of a number of documents that
set out the aspirations for future development in the local area.
These include core strategies, local development frameworks and
neighbourhood plans and are expressed in a written policy and
on proposals maps.

Development plans are individual to each LPA, but they are influenced by, and in some instances required to be compliant with, other legislation. The hierarchy for this is shown below. The development plan documents are in **bold**. All planning applications are determined in accordance with the development plan unless material considerations indicate otherwise (see page 22).

I European Spatial Directive – guidance
I National planning policy guidance
   o National Planning Policy Framework (NPPF)
   o Planning Practice Guidance (PPG)
   o Retained circulars and letters from the Chief Planner
I County/unitary authorities
   o **Saved policies**
   o **Core strategy**
   o **Minerals and waste development frameworks**
   o Supplementary guidance
I District/local plans
   o **Saved policies**
   o **Local development frameworks**
   o Supplementary guidance
I **Neighbourhood plans** (under localism)

Influencing the plan-making process

Plan making is a constantly evolving process, so to be effective in influencing changes requires a constant monitoring of draft plan development. Major clients and landowners will want to ensure that their interests are preserved and promoted by policy change so their agents will have to respond to emerging policy or proactively promote their clients' interests.

Local authorities are obliged to consult on the development of new plans. This process provides an opportunity for response to proposed policy changes at a relatively early stage. It is important that agents ensure that they are on the list of interested parties in order to receive notification of these consultations and that they monitor the timetable for plan development to identify when to promote their clients' interests. Objectors to new policies will be invited to make representations to the local plans examination conducted by the Planning Inspectorate. The Inspectorate will determine if the plan is 'sound'; this is set out in

Influencing plan policy – a major town extension

A world-leading university is a major employer and a defining identity of the city in which it has been located for many centuries. The reputation of the institution draws large donations and grants to extend the research facilities. As a result the number of research staff continues to grow, putting pressure on housing prices. New housing and research facilities can no longer be accommodated in the town and the university puts forward its research farmland outside the development boundary of the city for a new campus. The principle of development is included in the local development framework by the city council and the university enters into constructive discussions about the content of the action plan. Once the plan is adopted an outline application establishes the master plan for the site, and as each portion is brought forward for development reserved matters applications are made.

paragraph 182 of the National Planning Policy Framework (NPPF) under the headings of:

I Positively prepared
I Justified
I Effective
I Consistent with national policy.

Localism

The Localism Act 2011 allowed for the development of neighbourhood plans by local communities. These have to be broadly in line with the local plan or the emerging plan and to have undertaken a process of public examination and a local referendum before they are adopted. Once in place they are the only part of the development plan not produced by the planning authority. A neighbourhood plan should add detail to the local plan and represent the community's aspirations for development in their area. They are produced and approved by a process similar to that for Neighbourhood Development Orders.

The development of neighbourhood plans and other community engagement such as Neighbourhood Development Orders can provide architects and co-professionals with an opportunity to contribute their skills to provide a positive influence on their local environment while cementing their professional reputation in the area. The RIBA's *Guide to Localism* gives advice on getting involved.

Neighbourhood Development Order

Communities can use neighbourhood planning to permit development – in full or in outline – without the need for planning applications. This is achieved through the use of Neighbourhood Development Orders.

To come into force, proposed Neighbourhood Development Orders need to gain the approval of a majority of voters in a referendum of the neighbourhood. Before they can be put to a referendum they must:

- have regard to national planning policy
- be in general conformity with strategic policies in the development plan for the local area (such as in a core strategy)
- be compatible with EU obligations and human rights requirements.

This is checked by an independent qualified person.

If the proposals pass the referendum, the local planning authority is under a legal duty to bring them into force. The same process is adopted for approving neighbourhood plans.

Identifying development plan policies

As shown above, a development plan may have a number of components. It is important to assess whether any of these components include policies that will impact on the potential viability of the sites under consideration. Not all policies carry the same weight for the decision maker; the impact of these policies will be modified by their age and compliance with national policy. These considerations are set out on the following page:

Understanding the development plan legacy

Plans adopted pre 2004

If there is no post 2004 adopted plan there may be saved policies from an earlier plan. In 2012 the government abolished all outdated plans: all planning decisions were to be made in accordance with national guidance current at the time, and where no relevant policy existed the presumption in favour of sustainable development (see page 22) would apply. Local authorities could put forward policies to be saved in order to retain a framework for local decision making. These policies were assessed against government guidance and where they were compliant they were saved. These policies could be taken from:

– Regional Spatial Strategy
  The Regional Development Authorities were abolished by the Localism Act 2011. However, a few policies remain, including the Thames Basin Heaths Special Protection Area in the south-east, and the retention of the green belt around York from the Yorkshire and Humber Plan.
– County Council Structure Plans
  Two-tier authorities have complementary components of the development plan. The county component is largely strategic in intent and will include policies that set the context for more detailed policies in the local plan.
– Local plans
  The local plan will consist of the core strategy, written policies with supporting information on how the policy should be interpreted, and plans showing land allocation. If the area was under the control of a unitary authority, the local plan will also set out the strategic policies for the area.

Post 2004 Development Plans

Where post 2004 development plans have been adopted they form the development plan and supersede any saved policies. They can also include county structure plans for non-unitary authorities (areas with both a county council and borough or district council).

However, those written before 2012 were constructed on the basis of adding to, rather than repeating, government guidance. This guidance was abolished and replaced by the NPPF in March 2012, therefore many plans have been left without the more detailed support of the old Planning Policy Statements (PPSs) and older Planning Policy Guidance (PPG). Where the government's planning guidance has changed in emphasis or intent from the PPGs and PPSs it can have greater weight in decision making than a development plan based on the old guidance. This has been particularly apparent in housing policies as the government has attempted to loosen control over the siting of new development in order to stimulate the market and increase the rate at which new housing is constructed. In these situations the more restrictive local plan policy is considered out of date and the presumption in favour of sustainable development applies (see below).

Few local authorities had adopted post 2004 development plans when the NPPF was introduced in 2012. Since the introduction of the NPPF and a more streamlined plans approval process, many more have now been adopted.

Neighbourhood plans

Adopted neighbourhood plans all post-date the NPPF and unless there is an inadequate five-year land supply they will be given considerable weight by decision makers.

National policy

National policy is a material consideration that carries significant weight with decision makers, especially if the development plan is out of date and out of step with national intentions. There are two main vehicles for national policy:

National Planning Policy Framework

In March 2012 the Department for Communities and Local Government introduced the National Planning Policy Framework, which reduced over 1,000 pages of national policy to around 50. It abolished the national Planning Policy Statements and the earlier national Planning Policy Guidance notes.

Planning Practice Guidance

Online updated guidance was first issued in March 2014 by the government to underpin the National Planning Policy Framework. It carries the same weight for decision makers as the NPPF.

Presumption in favour of sustainable development

If a development plan is out of date – either because it pre-dates the NPPF and contradicts it or the information contained in a new plan is not current – the NPPF states that there is a presumption in favour of development if it is sustainable. Sustainability is defined in terms of economic, social and environmental dimensions. This 'golden thread' running through national policy makes it essentially in favour of schemes that comply with national policy and it compels local authorities to maintain their policy documents if they want to retain control of the siting of development.

How planning decisions are made

The key objective is to achieve planning consent for the proposed development, whether large or small, in a timely way and by an affordable route. From the outset the mindset of the decision maker needs to be understood and the strategic planning case established. This will determine whether the proposed development is viable and what material considerations are likely to apply to the application.

Rarely is an application covered solely by the development plan policies – more usually the plan is the starting point. Decision makers also have to take account of other factors that may operate for or against the granting of approval. These factors include material considerations and the harm that might be caused by the development. Establishing the material considerations and their implications for the project early in the process is essential to the success of the subsequent application or applications and ultimately to successful Project Outcomes.

Material considerations

Material considerations are matters relevant to planning that can be used to justify the approval of an application that goes against policies contained in the development plan. They can be negative as well as positive, so they can also be weighed against the benefits of a proposal. As they can influence the outcomes of applications and appeals, they are frequently tested in the courts. As a consequence, the list of material considerations is frequently amended. However, it can include:

l the development plan itself
l development factors, such as:
   o buildings: number, size, height, layout, siting, design and external appearance
   o site: access and highway safety, landscape, impact on character and appearance
   o neighbours: impact on existing and proposed living conditions
   o environment: ecology, archaeology, infrastructure, noise and other nuisance
l government policy
l emerging policies
l third party representations, including concerns about safety
l planning gain and Community Infrastructure Levy (see page 39)
l need, including economic and housing need
l enabling development (see page 60)
l ability of the LPA to impose conditions
l precedent
l personal circumstances (limited usually to green belt development)
l sustainability
l viability
l fallback position
l human rights, including the rights of the child.

Matters that are not considered material include:

l those regulated by other legislation, such as the building regulations and private rights to light
l objections on moral grounds
l the effect on property values
l views from private property
l protection of personal interests other than residential amenity
l legal restrictions, such as easement, wayleaves and covenants.

Public opinion can be enflamed by the prospect of development, but objections to a planning application need to meet normal criminal tests and not incite racial hatred or public disorder.

Harm

The decision maker has to identify whether the proposal would be harmful to the interests of the community and to society as a whole. It is useful to use accepted terminology for harm when setting out the case in support of a project. The sliding scale for harm is:

I Substantial
I Considerable
I Significant
I Some
I Modest
I Limited
I Little or no

The general test

In general planning areas the test is whether the proposal would cause any 'material or unacceptable harm to interests of acknowledged importance'. Some harm can be identified for most proposals, unless it is an improvement to an unacceptable existing situation and without any detracting features. For most proposals the harm is limited when weighed against material considerations that would be a benefit to the community.

Example of the balance of harm against benefit to the community

A new primary school is proposed on playing fields in a residential area. There are objections from local residents on the grounds of potential dangers to highway safety due to congestion and parking at school delivery and collection times and objections about noise nuisance from the playground. However, the school is needed to replace an inadequate Victorian building and the site is central to the catchment area, minimising impacts on traffic congestion and the need for school transport. The balance of the wider community need against the concerns of individuals is found to be compelling and the school is granted planning permission, but with conditions on travel management.

Areas of constraint

In areas of special designation the test for harm is higher and the probability of obtaining permission for new development consequently much diminished. It is important to determine from the outset if the sites under consideration in the Strategic Brief are in such an area as the planning implications could be very restrictive. The local plan should have maps indicating the policies that apply to a site or area. They will also show the development boundary of settlements. Local plan and national area designations will also be shown.

Areas of constraint

Areas recognised as having exceptional merit for natural or heritage reasons or needed to check the spread of development that are designated for a higher level of protection.

Areas and assets that are covered by national legislation and policies of constraint are:

I Natural environment
  o National Parks
  o The Broads
  o Areas of Outstanding Natural Beauty (AONB)
I Historic environment
  o conservation areas
  o listed buildings and ancient monuments
I Green belt

The natural environment

The NPPF sets out policy in relation to the natural environment at paragraph 115:

Paragraph 115 of the National Planning Policy Framework

Great weight should be given to conserving landscape and scenic beauty in National Parks, the Broads and Areas of Outstanding Natural Beauty, which have the highest status of protection in relation to landscape and scenic beauty. The conservation of wildlife and cultural heritage are important considerations in all these areas, and should be given great weight in National Parks and the Broads.

The test for harm here is that development should conserve or enhance the natural and local environment. There can be no development that will cause harm unless there are weighty material considerations that outweigh this harm.

Example of where harm outweighs material considerations

An application is made for an extension to a house in a prominent location in an Area of Outstanding Natural Beauty. The extension would take the form of a large wing to the house and would be considerably larger than permitted development rights would allow (see page 31). It would be visible from roads both adjacent to it and across the valley and would result in considerable impact on the character and appearance of the area, which the planning officer suggests would be harmful. The applicant has set out personal circumstances to justify both the form and the size of the extension. Her disabled son requires a swimming pool for necessary physiotherapy. Although sympathetic to the need, the planning inspector who determines the appeal decides that the life of the building will extend well beyond the needs of the existing occupiers and that the ongoing harm outweighs this material consideration.

Example of where harm is outweighed by material considerations

A development of five houses is proposed for an Area of Outstanding Natural Beauty immediately adjacent to a market town. The site is well screened and sited in the grounds of a former vicarage. The development would be slightly visible from the existing public highway and from a public footpath 500 metres away. The proposal is highly sustainable, both in terms of location and design. The market town lies within a borough in which 90% of the non-urban land area is either AONB or green belt. The council has failed to identify five years' supply of land to meet the need for new houses and as a consequence its policies requiring the siting of housing within existing settlement boundaries is considered not to be up to date and the presumption in favour of sustainable development applies (para. 49 of the NPPF). In deciding the approval the planning inspector has to balance the harm to the landscape and scenic beauty of the AONB against the need for new homes and determines that the appeal should be allowed.

The historic environment

For proposals in conservation areas and World Heritage Sites and for work that would affect listed buildings and ancient monuments there is a requirement to conserve and enhance the significance of heritage assets, a term that covers all these historical features. This includes the character and appearance of the asset and also its setting.

Legislation and policy for the historic environment

Works that affect listed buildings and conservation areas may require separate consent under the Planning (Listed Buildings and Conservation Areas) Act 1990. National policy for planning that affects these assets and their setting can be found in the NPPF at paragraphs 126 to 141.

Heritage asset

A building, monument, site, place, area or landscape identified as having a degree of significance meriting consideration in planning decisions.

The NPPF stresses that the approach should be proportionate both in the level of detail required from applicants to describe the significance of any assets (para. 128) and in the weight attributed to the need for conservation (para. 132). Where the development would lead to less than substantial harm to the significance of a designated asset the harm should be weighed against the public benefits of the proposal (para. 134).

Example of the balance of harm to a heritage asset against public benefit

The public payment desk in a grade II* listed town hall is accessed by a short flight of steps on a side elevation. Disabled access is from the far side of the building, through the council offices. The council propose to reconfigure the stone steps to include a ramp and handrail. While there will be some harm to the appearance of the building, it is considered less than substantial and outweighed by the public benefit of access.

Green belt

Green belt

Green belts are areas of constraint against development around major urban conurbations. The aim of green belt policy is to prevent urban sprawl by keeping land permanently open. Openness is defined as the absence of development.

The principles that define green belt policy are set out in NPPF paragraphs 79 and 80:

Green belt policy in the National Planning Policy Framework

79. The Government attaches great importance to Green Belts. The fundamental aim of Green Belt policy is to prevent urban sprawl by keeping land permanently open; the essential characteristics of Green Belts are their openness and their permanence.

80. Green Belt serves five purposes:

- to check the unrestricted sprawl of large built-up areas;
- to prevent neighbouring towns merging into one another;
- to assist in safeguarding the countryside from encroachment;
- to preserve the setting and special character of historic towns; and
- to assist in urban regeneration, by encouraging the recycling of derelict and other urban land.

The NPPF requires LPAs to give substantial weight to any harm to the green belt (para. 88). Most forms of development are considered inappropriate in the green belt and therefore by their very nature harmful. Other harm is also weighed against the development, such as harm to character and appearance and nuisances such as noise. The result is that there have to be considerable benefits in the form of material considerations to outweigh that harm. In such rare instances it is considered that very special circumstances apply.

The definition of inappropriate development is by exception. New buildings that are not considered inappropriate development are:

| buildings for agriculture and forestry
| facilities for outdoor sport and recreation and cemeteries, with some provisos
| limited extensions and alterations to existing buildings
| replacement of a building
| limited infilling in villages

l   limited affordable housing provision
l   redevelopment of brownfield sites where there is no greater impact
    on openness.

It must be borne in mind that green belts are not always open countryside,
but that the test of openness is one of intensity of development, which
has environmental as well as visual components.

Example of the balancing exercise in the green belt

A redundant petrol filling station beside a trunk road in the
green belt has established lawful uses for vehicle repair and
the storage and sale of caravans. There are a number of
buildings used as workshops and a small bungalow that is still
occupied. The buildings are all in a state of disrepair and overall
appearance is unsightly. The site is 300 metres from a large
village with a primary school and two shops. The local authority
has acknowledged that it has insufficient land supply to meet
housing need for the next five years. The proposed residential
development is designed to have a built volume less than the
total volume of all of the buildings and the caravans that could be
stationed on the site. There would be fewer vehicular movements
from the proposed new use than from the existing uses.
The planning officer's report balances the harm of inappropriate
development and the loss of employment and economic
benefits against the material considerations of housing need, the
sustainable location, improvement to character and appearance
and increase in openness due to the reduction in building volume
and less intensive use. The officer concludes that very special
circumstances exist and recommends approval.

Locally designated areas

Local designations may include:

l   Local green space
l   Coastal Change Management Areas
l   Nature Improvement Areas
l   Special Protection Areas and Special Areas of Conservation for wildlife
l   Air Quality Management Areas
l   non-designated heritage assets

I green corridors and wedges
I development areas identified for industrial, commercial and housing
I locally designated valued landscapes
I Areas of Special Control for advertising.

The restrictions that apply will be specific to the reasons for designation. The test for harm in these areas is not always as onerous as that for nationally designated areas (Special Protection Areas for wildlife are an exception to this as they can prevent all new housing development in an area). However, the designations are enshrined in the development plan, which is the starting point for the decision maker, and the material considerations that are put forward to outweigh the harm caused by developing against policy have to be sufficient to overcome that harm.

Permitted development

Not all development requires planning permission. Certain development and some changes of use are permitted. Permitted development rights are complex and apply to domestic properties and some agricultural, commercial and industrial buildings. The primary legislation is the Town and Country Planning (General Permitted Development) Order 1995 (GPDO); however, this has been amended many times.

Permitted development rights (PD rights)

These are classes of development for which a grant of planning permission is automatically given by national legislation, provided that no restrictive condition is attached or that the development is exempt.

Extensions are permitted provided that the allowance of additional volume has not previously been used up. Some detailed historical research may be required for older properties. The original size of the building is that which was in existence on 1 July 1948 if it was constructed before that date. If constructed after that date, the size will be what was originally approved. For up-to-date guidance on PD rights consult the Planning Portal at:

www.planningportal.gov.uk/permission/responsibilities/
planningpermission/permitted.

There have been temporary increases in the sizes of domestic extensions and agricultural barn conversions allowed under PD rights. For information on the current PD rights, the neighbour consultation scheme and the prior approval notice requirements, refer to the Planning Portal.

Article 4 directions may be in place in some areas, frequently conservation areas. These directions withdraw some or all of the automatic rights to approval under PD rights. They will be identified in the policy search. Areas of constraint, such as National Parks, Areas of Outstanding Natural Beauty and the Norfolk or Suffolk Broads, will also have restrictions on permitted development.

Local Development Orders can be put into place by a local authority. These are used to extend PD rights, usually in order to stimulate economic growth.

Change of use

There are two types of development that may require planning permission:

I Operational development: where there is some physical change, usually the erection of a building or an extension.
I Change of use: in such cases some minor building work may be incidental to that use.

For example, the change of use from an office to a shop may entail no external change except for a new bin store to the rear. Usually that work would not require planning permission as it is incidental to the new use.

Building uses are grouped into use classes. Changing use within a use class is allowed as permitted development. The GPDO is regularly amended so it is important to access the most recent information through the Planning Portal.

Use classes

The definition of use classes is given in the Town and Country Planning (Use Classes) Order 1987 as currently amended. The LPA should be consulted as to its definition of the use class of a particular existing or proposed use. The Planning Portal gives the following guidance:

Definition of use classes

A1 Shops – Shops, retail warehouses, hairdressers, undertakers, travel and ticket agencies, post offices (but not sorting offices), pet shops, sandwich bars, showrooms, domestic hire shops, dry cleaners, funeral directors and internet cafés.

A2 Financial and professional services – Financial services such as banks and building societies, professional services (other than health and medical services) including estate and employment agencies and betting offices.

A3 Restaurants and cafés – For the sale of food and drink for consumption on the premises – restaurants, snack bars and cafés.

A4 Drinking establishments – Public houses, wine bars or other drinking establishments (but not night clubs).

A5 Hot food takeaways – For the sale of hot food for consumption off the premises.

B1 Business – Offices (other than those that fall within A2), research and development of products and processes, light industry appropriate in a residential area.

B2 General industrial – Use for industrial process other than one falling within class B1 (excluding incineration purposes, chemical treatment or landfill or hazardous waste).

B8 Storage or distribution – This class includes open air storage.

C1 Hotels – Hotels, boarding and guest houses where no significant element of care is provided (excludes hostels).

C2 Residential institutions – Residential care homes, hospitals, nursing homes, boarding schools, residential colleges and training centres.

C2A Secure Residential Institution – Use for a provision of secure residential accommodation, including use as a prison, young offenders institution, detention centre, secure training centre, custody centre, short term holding centre, secure hospital, secure local authority accommodation or use as a military barracks.

Definition of use classes (*continued*)

C3 Dwellinghouses – this class is formed of 3 parts:

C3(a) covers use by a single person or a family (a couple whether married or not, a person related to one another with members of the family of one of the couple to be treated as members of the family of the other), an employer and certain domestic employees (such as an au pair, nanny, nurse, governess, servant, chauffeur, gardener, secretary and personal assistant), a carer and the person receiving the care and a foster parent and foster child.

C3(b) up to six people living together as a single household and receiving care e.g. supported housing schemes such as those for people with learning disabilities or mental health problems.

C3(c) allows for groups of people (up to six) living together as a single household. This allows for those groupings that do not fall within the C4 HMO definition, but which fell within the previous C3 use class, to be provided for i.e. a small religious community may fall into this section as could a homeowner who is living with a lodger.

C4 Houses in multiple occupation – small shared houses occupied by between three and six unrelated individuals, as their only or main residence, who share basic amenities such as a kitchen or bathroom.

D1 Non-residential institutions – Clinics, health centres, crèches, day nurseries, day centres, schools, art galleries (other than for sale or hire), museums, libraries, halls, places of worship, church halls, law court. Non residential education and training centres.

D2 Assembly and leisure – Cinemas, music and concert halls, bingo and dance halls (but not night clubs), swimming baths, skating rinks, gymnasiums or area for indoor or outdoor sports and recreations (except for motor sports, or where firearms are used).

Sui Generis – Certain uses do not fall within any use class and are considered 'sui generis'. Such uses include: theatres, houses in multiple occupation, hostels providing no significant element of care, scrap yards. Petrol filling stations and shops selling and/ or displaying motor vehicles. Retail warehouse clubs, nightclubs, launderettes, taxi businesses, amusement centres and casinos.

Source: The Planning Portal

Table 0.1   Changes of use not requiring planning permission

FROM	TO
A2 (professional and financial services) when premises have a display window at ground level	**A1** (shop)
A3 (restaurants and cafés)	**A1** or **A2**
A4 (drinking establishments)	**A1** or **A2** or **A3**
A5 (hot food takeaways)	**A1** or **A2** or **A3**
B1 (business) (permission limited to change of use relating to not more than 500 square metres of floor space)	**B8** (storage and distribution)
B2 (general industrial)	**B1** (business)
B2 (general industrial) (permission limited to change of use relating to not more than 500 square metres of floor space)	**B8** (storage and distribution)
B8 (storage and distribution) (permission limited to change of use relating to not more than 500 square metres of floor space)	**B1** (business)
C3 (dwellinghouses)	**C4** (houses in multiple occupation)
C4 (houses in multiple occupation)	**C3** (dwellinghouses)
Casinos (sui generis)	**D2** (assembly and leisure)

Source: The Planning Portal

Change of use

Some changes of use between use classes are permitted development. This is where the impact of the new use will be less than that of the existing use (eg changing a casino to other assembly and leisure uses) or where the benefits and impacts are similar (eg changing a dwelling-house to a house in multiple occupation). This reduces unnecessary red tape and the consequent impacts on businesses.

There are additional permitted changes and the situation changes regularly. The Planning Portal carries information on the permanent and temporary changes to the GPDO.

Betterment

Betterment occurs when a new development will potentially have a lower impact on a site or area than the current use. The current use of

Example of betterment in negotiation of change of use

A new residential development is proposed for a redundant livestock market located outside the development boundary. Although it has not been used for several years the planning case assesses the vehicle movements and the type of vehicles that would be used to serve a market on three days a week, including the peak flow times before and after the sale. It also assesses the likely impact of lighting, noise and smell on residents in the area. These are weighed against the vehicle movements associated with a residential development and their peak flows and any other possible nuisances to the existing residents. Clearly, the proposed scheme represents betterment over the existing use.

the site can therefore have a significant role in the negotiation of change of use, particularly when the proposal is outside policy. Whether or not the site is currently used for its defined planning use, the potential or real impact of the use can be weighed against the potential impact of the proposed scheme.

Secretary of State 'call-in'

If a local authority proposes to approve an application that is a departure from its local development plan it must notify the Secretary of State, who can elect to call it in to determine it by public inquiry. The Secretary of State can call in any application at any stage of the process; however, this rarely happens, and is usually reserved for matters of national significance.

The planning process – impacts on Project Programme and Project Budget

Project Programme

Although the target time requirements of the planning process are set out by the Secretary of State (detailed on page 109: Stage 3), the project lead needs to be mindful of the potential for delay before, during and after the application process. The project lead should make the client aware of this uncertainty in the programme and their lack of control over the LPA's performance.

The potential delays can be mitigated by effective pre-application consultation, which should determine what information is required to support the application and what expectations the LPA has of the scheme (see page 67: Stage 1). However, this is subject to the interpretation of individual officers and the advice given at pre-application meetings is not binding on the authority. The project lead will therefore also need to make the client aware of the risk of inaccurate advice from the LPA.

An indication of the minimum timescales that should be allowed in the programme for planning-related activities is given in figure 0.1. The design and preparation time will vary from project to project.

Project Budget

Planning impacts on the Project Budget in a number of ways; these can be summarised as the costs of:

I preparing the application, usually fees for reports and surveys required for validation
I mitigation to reduce identified harm
I public consultation
I delay in obtaining planning permission
I planning obligations and Community Infrastructure Levy
I additional investigations and design to support conditions applications.

These are covered in detail in subsequent chapters and are usually estimated for the purposes of the Stage 0 Strategic Brief and Business Case. However, of significance at this stage are the costs of planning obligations and the Community Infrastructure Levy, which can be significant amounts within the Project Budget and impact on the financial viability of the Business Case.

Section 106 planning obligations

As the name suggests these are legislated for in section 106 of the Town and Country Planning Act 1990. They cover a range of legal agreements that make an otherwise unacceptable proposal acceptable to the LPA (see page 110: Stage 3). They are frequently used to:

I secure the provision of affordable housing
I restrict the development or use of the land in any specified way

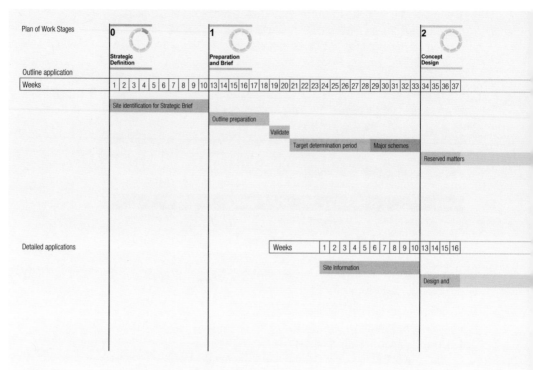

Figure 0.1   Sample programme for planning applications

I   require specified operations or activities
I   require the land to be used in any specified way
I   require a sum or sums to be paid to the authority.

Source: Planning Advisory Service

For housing development the requirement to provide affordable housing on a site would reduce the return to the developer for the plots allocated to the registered social landlord and could reduce the market value of the whole development. The requirement therefore needs to be considered in the Business Case. A typical requirement will be for 20% affordable housing in developments of ten or more units. The Growth and Infrastructure Act 2013 introduced a right of appeal over section 106 obligations that relate to the provision of affordable housing in order to make some existing approvals commercially viable.

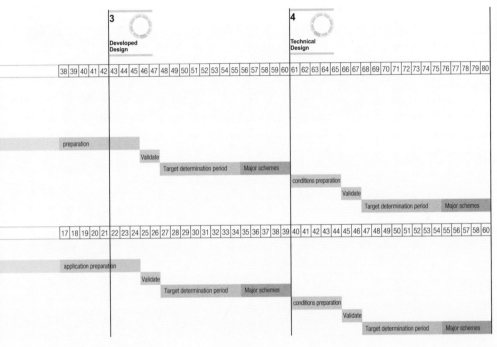

Sums of money can be required as a 'developer's contribution'. According to paragraph 201 of the NPPF, these monies have to be:

I necessary to make the development acceptable in planning terms
I directly related to the development
I fairly and reasonably related in scale and kind to the development.

An indication of the amount of any contribution should be provided by the LPA during pre-application consultations.

Community Infrastructure Levy

Community Infrastructure Levy (CIL) was introduced in the 2008 Planning Act as the government felt that section 106 agreements were not meeting the wider infrastructure consequences of new development. The method of calculating CIL and the types of development that it applies to vary from

Plot finding

Practices may be called upon to advise on a number of sites and proposals before a site is purchased for a new home, conversion or renovation project. Part of this advice will be on any planning constraints or opportunities, including whether planning permission will not be required at all under permitted development rights.

LPA to LPA. The introduction of the charging regime is subject to public consultation and at the time of writing not all LPAs have provisions for CIL in place. Once in place the rates are transparent and should make budgeting more accurate than assessing possible section 106 liabilities. However, CIL does not replace all contributions required by section 106 agreements, so advice from the LPA will still be necessary.

Devising a planning strategy

Ultimately the planning officer's report will assess the development plan and all relevant material considerations. When preparing the planning report for the Strategic Brief it is helpful to set out all the identified implications, as far as they can be predicted, to compare different sites and proposals. They may have considerable impact on the viability of the options under consideration, affecting the Business Cases for the proposals. A summary is shown in table 0.2.

The Strategic Brief may contain assessments for a number of options or identify and analyse one site and development proposal. The client's risk profile should be reflected in the recommendations for taking each proposal forward. With the opportunities and constraints identified, the report should recommend early actions to prepare the case and minimise delay at the application stage.

Table 0.2   Summary of strategic planning considerations

CONSIDERATIONS FOR DEVELOPMENT	CONSIDERATIONS AGAINST DEVELOPMENT	PROJECT BUDGET AND PROJECT PROGRAMME IMPLICATIONS
EXISTING BUILDINGS		
Extensions		
Permitted development rights Enabling development Character and appearance Economic benefits for client and wider community	Listed building Area of constraint harms: character and appearance, openness Intensification of use harm, eg highways and parking, residential amenity Planning gain and CIL on larger extensions	May not need planning approval Increased level of specification: very detailed scheme required for applications Good design may increase chances of gaining approval Local opposition may delay approval Impact of charges on the Business Case
Refurbishment and alteration		
Internal works may not require planning	Listed building consent may be required	May not need consent
Change of use		
Permitted development rights Betterment	Intensification of use harm, eg highways and parking, residential amenity	May not need planning approval Local opposition may delay approval Validation requirements could add cost and delay
NEW BUILDINGS		
Character and appearance Sustainability Betterment Economic need Housing need National policy	Area of constraint harms: character and appearance, openness Development factors: buildings, site, neighbours, environment Planning gain and CIL on larger extensions	Good design may increase chances of gaining approval Validation requirements could add cost and delay Local opposition may delay approval Impact of charges on the Business Case

Chapter summary   0

The new Stage 0 of the RIBA Plan of Work 2013 provides the opportunity for clients and their advisers to test the feasibility of the options under consideration, which includes identifying the planning opportunities and constraints and relating these to the Business Case and Strategic Brief. The planning strategy that underpins the viable business case forms part of the Strategic Brief.

An effective assessment cannot be undertaken without an understanding of the roles that policy and the statutory process play in determining the outcome of a planning application. This must be supplemented with understanding and experience of the pragmatic realities of the system in order to be able to give a realistic prediction of the likely planning outcomes for the project.

Preparation and Brief

Chapter overview

At this stage of the Plan of Work the preparatory work for the planning submission commences with the collation of Site Information and preparation of Feasibility Studies. These inform pre-application discussions with the planning authority, which contribute to the development of the Initial Project Brief including review of the Project Budget and the Project Programme. Actions at this stage can include obtaining certificates of lawful use, lawful development certificates and making outline applications.

The key coverage in this chapter is as follows:

Assembling Site Information

Identifying the planning context

Submitting applications to establish use or the principle of development

Identifying other relevant legislation

Conducting pre-application discussions

Identifying validation requirements

Preparing a Stage 1 Site Information and planning report

Introduction

This chapter covers those elements of the Initial Project Brief that are derived from the Site Information. Understanding the site and its potential for development has implications for the project beyond planning, and although the main focus is on planning matters, the wider information required is also covered in this chapter.

Obtaining planning permission can be a significant hurdle to overcome. Delay is a possible, sometimes inevitable, part of the process and failure to gain approval will put the whole project in jeopardy. Understanding the planning context for the site and project is essential to minimise these risks. However, a thorough investigation of the planning context can also lead to the identification of other opportunities for the development. It is therefore important to prepare the case well to minimise risk and maximise benefits. Early contact with the local planning authority should establish what supporting information may be required to support an application and therefore what consultants will need to be appointed to prepare the relevant reports. This can take time and needs to be factored into the Project Budget and Project Programme. On larger projects a Stage 1 planning report encapsulating the Site Information obtained and the proposed planning strategy will be prepared as part of the Initial Project Brief.

What are the Core Objectives of this stage?

The Core Objectives of the RIBA Plan of Work 2013 at Stage 1 are:

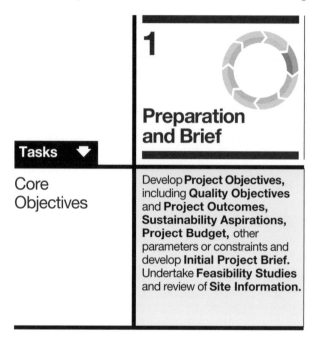

Tasks ▼	**1** Preparation and Brief
Core Objectives	Develop **Project Objectives**, including **Quality Objectives** and **Project Outcomes, Sustainability Aspirations, Project Budget,** other parameters or constraints and develop **Initial Project Brief.** Undertake **Feasibility Studies** and review of **Site Information.**

The Initial Project Brief will contain the parameters and constraints identified in the Site Information and a planning report setting out how the Project Objectives will be achieved in terms of the planning strategy. This will include the implications for the Project Budget and Project Programme of any site and planning constraints.

Assembling Site Information

Good quality Site Information is a core objective for the project. The stages at which the information is obtained will vary and assumptions based on experience may have to be taken by the lead designer if incomplete information is available at Stage 1. In some circumstances, for example where a client has an option on a site pending successful planning consent, the client may not wish to commission every survey at Stage 1.

Sources of Site Information can be:

I desktop survey
I visual Inspection
I topographical survey
I buildings surveys
I soil investigation
I specialist environmental surveys
I engineering reports
I archaeological surveys.

Some or all of these may be required to substantiate a planning application or listed building consent application. The validation requirements and the impacts on Project Budget and Project Programme are set out in table 1.1 (page 71).

Desktop surveys

The desktop survey can provide a significant depth of detail prior to site-based investigations. It will give a strong indication of what further investigations may need to be commissioned both for the Concept Design and Developed Design stages and for planning validation purposes.

Desktop studies might comprise:

Desktop studies

- General context, character, outstanding features
- Land ownership
- Detrimental local features
- Planning policy context
- Historic environment
- Contaminated Land Register
- Coal Board records
- Traffic conditions
- Planned works to the highway
- Previous site history – possible contaminants etc.
- Archaeology
- Designations under the Wildlife and Countryside Act 1981
- Flooding
- Tree Preservation Orders
- Rights of way
- Services, overground and underground
- Proposed use: special requirements for fire safety, public health, Building Control
- Statutory bodies
- Levels, benchmarks

Much of the desktop study can be undertaken by the lead designer, whose initial search will reveal where further investigation by specialists is required. The specialist investigations need to be added to the Project Execution Plan and included on the Project Roles Table and the specialists' roles identified in the Schedule of Services. If further requirements are

Sources of data for desktop surveys

- Planning Portal: at planningportal.gov.uk/
- Local planning authority websites
- Google search, especially for local history
- Google Earth
- English Heritage: at list.english-heritage.org.uk/
- Environment Agency: at maps.environment-agency.gov.uk/
- Magic Maps, for historic and natural environment: at magic.defra.gov.uk/
- Land Registry

identified through negotiations with the planning authority or from unforeseen conditions, these will need to be amended and additional fees added to the Project Budget.

Visual inspection

It is essential to visit the site to gain an accurate impression of its condition and context. Site visits should be made in good light and, in the case of long-running landscape-based issues, in both winter and summer months. It is unlikely that all members of the team will visit the site in the early stages, therefore sketches and photographs are important for communicating the conditions to the project team. It is helpful to have a generic checklist for all initial site visits to ensure that key details are not overlooked.

Visual inspection checklist

- Aspect: orientation, shelter, overshadowing (buildings, hills and trees)
- Prospect: key views
- Hydrology: rivers, streams, ditches, ponds, wet/soft patches, underground watercourses, wells and springs, evidence of flooding, site levels relative to watercourses
- Vegetation: trees (approximate height, spread and girth), hedges, ground cover, roots, condition of each
- Topographical and geological features: slopes, rock outcrops, evidence of fault lines, coal
- Services: overhead cables, pylons, poles, marker posts, cover-plates (water, telecoms), manholes, governors, substations, hydrants
- Climate: frost and fog pockets, local wind conditions
- Health and safety hazards: flooding, highways, unsafe trees, overhead cables, old structures above and below ground, structural stability, rot, birds and bats
- Adjoining properties: condition, use, subsidence, fire risks, party walls, access and access rights, incoming and outgoing services, boundary encroachment, building lines
- Evidence of previous uses: buildings, substructure, car parking, boundary treatments, archaeology, burials
- Architectural context: building styles, materials
- Adjacent thoroughfares: waterways, railways, roads, footpaths, sightlines and forward visibility
- Access restrictions: adjacent uses, physical constraints, time constraints
- Sensitive adjacent uses: hospital, schools, law court, residents, hazardous commercial
- Possible nuisance: odour, noise (including night-time), overlooking, overbearing

After the site visit and the desktop survey an analysis can be made of any additional site-specific investigations and surveys that will be necessary for an accurate assessment of the site in order to minimise risks. These should be added to the agreed Information Exchange if not included in the original agreement. The following surveys may then be commissioned at this stage.

Topographical surveys

Topographical surveys measure the size, shape and features of a site. Laser technology is utilised to produce 2D and 3D CAD (computer-aided design) models, which are essential for accurate dimensioning and location of the proposed development. If the survey is delayed until Stage 2 the lack of dimensional accuracy needs to be noted on all feasibility studies prepared at Stage 1.

Topographical survey checklist

- Grid of levels relative to a local datum or to the national datum (necessary for flood risk areas to prepare a flood risk assessment)
- Contours at defined intervals
- Boundaries and boundary features
- Site features: water courses, rock outcrops
- Locations of buildings on the site and adjacent to the site
- Heights of buildings on and adjacent to the site and positions of any overlooking windows (necessary for rights to light and privacy issues)
- Locations of visible services on and adjacent to site, overhead services
- Drainage cover levels and invert levels
- Trees: height, spread and girth (necessary to establish root protection areas)
- Access: vertical clearance and forward visibility
- Adjacent highway features: junctions, width constraints, pavements and street furniture

Building surveys

There are two types of building survey: measured and condition.

Measured surveys

These can be carried out using a handheld laser and drawn up as a CAD drawing. For larger, more complex buildings, photogrammetry and point cloud surveys can be used, particularly to capture external elevations where accurate measurement is not possible from the ground. Generally, a building survey needs to contain sufficient information to facilitate proposals to refurbish, convert, alter or extend and will show plan and section information, including the relationship to outside levels.

Surveys of listed buildings

Accurate surveys and photographic records are an essential part of a listed building application. The survey of a listed building will need to include internal and external architectural details.

Condition surveys

These surveys cover the conditions of the fabric of a structure and can be a combination of visual inspection and invasive investigation.

Conditions survey checklist

- Damp
- Rot and moulds
- Insect infestation
- Structural instability and subsidence (a separate structural engineer's report may be required)
- Non-standard structures and fabric
- Asbestos (this is a specialist investigation and suspected asbestos should not be disturbed)
- Services (specialist surveys from services engineers may be required)

Building surveys for small practices

⌂

Building conditions surveys, particularly structural surveys, may be excluded from standard small practice professional indemnity cover so this must be checked before offering any advice on the condition of a building. This applies to casual advice as well as commissioned reports. For more detailed commentary, see *Good Practice Guide: Building Condition Surveys* by Mike Hoxley.

Soil investigation

Information about ground conditions can give early indications of the likely foundation type required. Ground conditions can be a major uncertainty in the Project Budget. A thorough investigation can reduce contingencies against this element of the building and permit accurate budgeting and programming.

Surveys can include:

I desktop survey of underling geology and site history
I trial pits and trenches for shallow investigations
I probes and boreholes for deeper investigations.

Samples extracted can be subjected to laboratory testing to determine factors such as bearing capacity and water content. These surveys are specialist activities, but the results can be key to developing an accurate Initial Project Brief. If they are delayed until Stage 2, an appropriate contingency should be shown in both the Project Brief and the Project Budget.

Specialist environmental surveys

There are numerous surveys and assessments that may be required to support a valid planning application (see table 1.1, page 71). Every site is different and an early identification of the supporting information that will be required will prevent unnecessary delay before an application can be submitted. For example, some ecological studies are seasonal in nature, such as identifying summer and winter bat roosts, which means an application may have to be delayed until they are completed. If identified early the survey can be conducted during Stages 1 and 2 and be ready for submission with the detailed application in Stage 3. If the need for a specialist report is suspected or the local planning authority (LPA) indicates that one would be required for validation, this should be added to the planning strategy as early as Stage 0. Such reports can include assessments and surveys for:

I air quality
I arboriculture
I biodiversity
I environmental impact
I heritage
I highways
I land contamination
I landscape and visual impact
I noise and vibration.

Some mitigation work can commence ahead of obtaining planning approval; for example, relocating species such as slow-worms. In extreme circumstances, some issues, such as air pollution or noise, may prevent development altogether, so early identification is essential to prevent abortive work.

Engineering reports

These can be commissioned early, both to inform the Initial Project Brief and to form part of the supporting documentation for the planning submission:

I drainage
I flood risk
I structure.

Again issues identified in engineering reports can threaten the viability of the project, so early identification is essential.

Archaeological surveys

Where the desktop investigation has identified the possibility of significant archaeological remains and pre-application discussions with the LPA have indicated that a pre-commencement excavation will be required, a limited survey may confirm the presence of remains and inform the Initial Project Brief to allow the time for additional investigation work to be factored into the Project Programme. (For pre-commencement conditions, see page 127: Stage 4.)

Identifying the planning context

A key activity in the desktop study is to establish the planning context for the site and the proposed project. This should be carried out before commencing pre-application discussions with the local LPA in order to ensure the discussion focuses on the relevant issues.

Planning history

The LPA will list previous applications (and their outcomes) for the site and adjacent sites for the past decade on its website. Earlier applications may have to be retrieved from the archive and viewed at the LPA's offices, where notes or copies can be made. There is usually a charge for copying. Previous applications will fall into one of three categories:

I approved and built
I approved and not built
I refused.

How to interpret planning history – approved and built applications

The history of previous approvals will reveal what has been constructed on the site as permitted development and what was built in accordance with planning consents. Two issues to identify are:

– **Existing conditions**
Examination of past approvals may identify unfulfilled conditions that could transfer with ownership of the site and become a liability through enforcement. This is usually carried out as part of the searches conducted on the purchase of the site, but it may be useful to the client if the risks can be identified ahead of the searches being returned.

– **Permitted development**
A search of existing approvals can also identify where there is capacity to extend an existing building in accordance with permitted development rights (see page 31: Stage 0). This can be important where an increase in the volume of the building is proposed, either by extending an existing building or redeveloping the site. It can be particularly important in green belt areas, where local plan policies may restrict the total volume of granted extensions over and above permitted development. Permitted development rights can be traded-in as part of the negotiation for a larger building on the site. It should be established whether conditions placed on a previous application have removed permitted development rights which will mean that planning permission will be needed for all or specified alterations and extensions.

How to interpret planning history – approved and not built applications

Applications for planning consent on the site or adjacent sites that have been approved but not carried out may give an indication of what may be acceptable to the LPA in a future application. The conditions imposed on these consents may also give an indication of the relevant issues. However, these should be approached with caution, especially if they are not recent, as they may have been consented in an earlier policy environment or the context of the site may have changed; for example, a previously existing need may have already been met by subsequent development.

How to interpret planning history – previously refused applications

It is important to examine applications for development or change of use for the site and adjacent sites that may have been refused, both by the LPA and at appeal. For LPA refusals the decision notice and the planning officer's report to the planning committee will give an indication of the issues that would have to be addressed by subsequent proposals for the site. However, it is important to be aware of the policy context in which the decision was reached.

– **Has the principle of development been established?**
It is difficult to gain consent for development that is similar to a proposed development on the same site that has been refused and upheld at appeal. However, it is worth studying the planning inspector's decision letter as they may have dismissed some of the LPA's reasons for refusal and established that the principle of the development is acceptable. If a subsequent application addresses the outstanding issues in a satisfactory way there is every reason to believe that it may be granted consent.

– **Changes in policy and guidance**
The date of the refusal should be considered and the impact of changes in the planning policy context taken into account. In some areas, the National Planning Policy Framework (NPPF) is more permissive than older development plan policies. For example, paragraph 47 of the NPPF requires LPAs to identify a current five-year land supply for housing development. If the LPA is unable to do this then local plan policies restricting new housing to within development boundaries are not in accordance with national planning guidance. As paragraph 49, states the 'presumption in favour of sustainable development' applies. The LPA is then required to consider all sustainable sites brought forward by developers in order to meet its housing need.

Paragraph 49 of the National Planning Policy Framework

Housing applications should be considered in the context of the presumption in favour of sustainable development. Relevant policies for the supply of housing should not be considered up-to-date if the local planning authority cannot demonstrate a five-year supply of deliverable housing sites.

Establishing use

The principle of use is important in planning. Permission is needed for change of use as well as for actual development, so establishing the existing and the proposed use classes is an important aspect of preparing the planning brief.

Establishing existing use

The existing uses of the site and any existing buildings should be established, whether they are current uses of the site or the site is redundant. This determines whether change of use will be a component of any planning application and what the fallback position would be if change of use is not granted.

It may not always be apparent what the current planning use of a site is and the planning history may have to be interrogated. If no consent for change has been given since 1 July 1948 the deemed use will be as it was at that date. This can be difficult to establish, but the LPA should be able to provide this information from the rating history of the site and other records.

Local plan policies

Identification of the relevant planning policies is key to determining the planning case and formulating the planning strategy.

General policy environment

The possible components of a development plan are set out on page 17: Stage 0. The policies that are relevant to the site and the proposal should be identified from these, along with any supplementary guidance. The policy environment will be a key element in determining the planning strategy, which, in turn, is a key element of the Initial Project Brief.

The planning history may provide some indication of the policies that the LPA considers to be relevant to the site. These may be found in planning officers' reports for previous applications, but it would be unwise to limit the search to this source. The proposed development may meet other policy requirements or address a need of national government or of the local community that has not been expressed in policy; an example would be a new prison. Material considerations such as these could be seen to outweigh failure to meet other policies. See page 24 (Stage 0) on the balancing exercise.

An example of when consent may be granted contrary to policy is an approval for enabling development, where a consent is given for a project that will release resources for a wider benefit.

Example of consent approved for enabling development

A hotel in a grade II* listed building is facing considerable costs for sensitive repairs and renovation. Consent is given for a large conservatory in the rear garden to enable the hotel to gain a wedding licence and increase its revenue, which in turn will support the costs of maintaining the building.

Special area designations

Once a site has been identified, area designations – both local and national, such as National Park, Area of Outstanding Natural Beauty or conservation area – that apply to the site and the surrounding area should be considered, and any balancing exercise of harm against benefit should be set out and assessed (see pages 26–27: Stage 0).

Green belt

The implications of a green belt area designation are discussed on pages 28–30 (Stage 0).

When preparing the planning case, the implications of proposing development in a green belt should be weighed against the particular circumstances of the site and local needs.

Historic environment

When a site has been identified it will be possible to assess the implications of historic environment designations on the proposed development. These are set out on page 27: Stage 0.

Submitting applications to establish use or the principle of development

The planning strategy may identify that an early application is desirable in order to establish a use or the principle of development. This may be achieved by making an outline application or by obtaining one of the certificates described below.

Outline application

An outline application contains only some of the information that will be required for full planning approval of the proposed development; it reserves a number of matters to be approved in a subsequent reserved matters application (see page 100: Stage 4). The outline application can be a simple red-line plan with all matters reserved. The Planning Portal defines reserved matters as follows:

I Appearance: aspects of a building or place which affect the way it looks, including the exterior of the development.
I Means of access: covers accessibility for all routes to and within the site, as well as the way they link up to other roads and pathways outside the site.
I Landscaping: the improvement or protection of the amenities of the site and the area and the surrounding area, this could include planting trees or hedges as a screen.
I Layout: includes buildings, routes and open spaces within the development and the way they are laid out in relation to buildings and spaces outside the development.
I Scale: includes information on the size of the development, including the height, width and length of each proposed building.

However, European environmental legislation requires that the planning authority knows enough about a development proposal to ascertain whether an environmental impact assessment is required, which can lead it to request more details. It may be expedient to determine some matters, such as means of access, if they are critical to the success of the final scheme. Applying for outline consent and then reserved matters has a significant effect on the Project Programme, but it may be necessary if the land is to be sold on to a developer with the benefit of consent.

Lawful development certificate

If permitted development rights are to be relied upon in the planning case the LPA should be asked for its interpretation of the rules pertaining to the proposed development at the pre-application meeting. A lawful development certificate can be obtained confirming that the existing or proposed work is permitted development, which will be helpful for future development on the site or when the client sells the property on.

Example of use of a lawful development certificate

The owners of a country house have two holiday cottages in the grounds that they wish to sell off as separate dwellings. This will require the removal of the conditions on the original approval that restricted the use of the cottages to holiday lets and the construction of a separate driveway through the grounds away from the main house. The LPA has suggested that the driveway could be constructed as permitted development but is opposing the lifting of the conditions. Before the case is made about the conditions, a lawful development certificate is applied for to secure the driveway in principle to prevent it becoming an issue in the subsequent application.

Certificate of lawfulness of existing use or development (CLEUD)

If the use of the site has changed in the past without planning consent and the site has constantly remained in that use ever since, a certificate of lawfulness of existing use or development, or CLEUD, can be applied for. A CLEUD can also be used to establish lawfulness if a condition was not complied with or buildings were erected without consent. It may be helpful to establish lawful use or development before making the case for the development proposal because it could establish precedent or assist the case for betterment.

The following periods of time have to elapse before the CLEUD can be applied for:

I 4 years for the erection of buildings or structures
I 4 years for the change of use of a building to a single dwelling
I 10 years for the change of use (building or land) to any use other than a single dwelling.

The certificate is not the grant of consent, rather it is a certification that the use or development is lawful. Note that use of land without planning permission is not illegal because, unless trespass is involved, it is not a criminal act, rather it is a civil offence. Evidence is required to enable the LPA to establish on the balance of probabilities that the use or development has met the prescribed timescales. This evidence could be council tax bills, electoral register, utility bills, accounts, photographs and signed affidavits from people with direct knowledge of the facts.

There have been high-profile cases of attempts to conceal development until the requisite period has elapsed and in April 2012 the government introduced new provisions for the enforcement of concealed breaches of planning control within section 124 of the Localism Act 2011, setting out new time limits for enforcing concealed breaches of planning control.

Case example of concealment

Fidler v Secretary of State for Communities and Local Government [2010] EWHC 143 (Admin)

The appellant built a house behind straw bales and tarpaulin without planning permission, intending to live in it for four years. The LPA, Reigate and Banstead Borough Council, served an enforcement notice requiring the house to be demolished, which the owner appealed on the grounds that he had established a lawful development after four years. The planning inspector and the high court found that the building had not been completed because the straw bales had not been removed and this had always been the intention of the appellant. The enforcement notice was upheld, requiring the building to be demolished.

Identifying other relevant legislation

Although this guide is primarily concerned with planning it should be noted that the site investigation should also include consideration of other property law that may impact on the proposed development and should be considered in the Initial Project Brief. It is particularly important to the planning case if it conflicts with planning requirements. For example, rights to light by neighbouring properties may suggest a built form at variance to a design brief or code from the LPA.

Consideration should be given to the implications of the following:

I Rights to light
The owner of a building with windows that have received natural daylight for 20 years or more can prevent any development that would reduce the light received. Permission can be sought to reduce daylight, but this cannot be presumed and so the Strategic Brief may include this as a design constraint.

I Easements
These are rights over another party's property and can include rights of way. They can be established by long use of the land and are shown on the title deeds for the land. Although they can be re-sited or removed by consent, the Initial Project Brief will have to give consideration to the

time that would be taken to do this; it may conclude that they should remain in place and be addressed as a site constraint.

I Wayleaves
These permit services to pass over or under land and usually include a safe working or loading envelope. The original agreement may be time limited and they can also be renegotiated, but if diversion is to be requested, the time for agreement and for the work to be carried out must be factored into the Project Programme. If this is considered too onerous, the route will have to be retained as a site constraint.

I Covenants
These are restrictions on the land placed by previous owners. Defunct covenants can be struck down by the Lands Tribunal, or an insurance policy can be bought to indemnify the new owners against someone coming forward to enforce the covenant. An example of a defunct covenant recently came to light in Essex: a cottage for sale was found to possess a covenant that restricted any occupiers from salting pork in the lounge. Live covenants can be recent and may restrict certain uses for the land or restrict overlooking. These take precedent over any planning approval and can only be removed by legal agreement. There will need to be a strategic decision to either negotiate or, if possible, design around the constraint. There may be a conflict with planning requirements that needs to be identified through pre-application discussion.

I Nuisance
The definition of a nuisance is something that is harmful or annoying to others, either as individuals (private nuisance) or the general public (public nuisance). Statutory nuisance is nuisance covered by the Environmental Protection Act 1990, which places an obligation on local authorities to investigate and, if necessary, enforce against certain types of nuisance. Nuisance can have implications for the proposed use of the land, either because it would cause a nuisance or because an existing adjacent use would not be compatible with the proposed use. Although not a planning matter, potential nuisance can be cited as a reason for refusing permission. Validation requirements may include assessments of noise, air quality or lighting to determine if there will be an issue and what mitigation is needed.

Statutory nuisance

The following issues constitute statutory nuisances:

- noise
- artificial light
- odour
- insects
- smoke
- dust
- premises
- fumes or gases
- accumulation or deposit
- animals kept in such a place or manner as to be prejudicial to health or a nuisance
- any other matter declared by any enactment to be a statutory nuisance.

Source: www.gov.uk/statutory-nuisance

Example of statutory nuisance considerations in a planning application

Southwark Council refused planning approval for a residential development at Elephant and Castle after an objection from the Ministry of Sound nightclub. The club feared that the residents would object to the night-time noise and use the Environmental Protection Act to close the club down. The decision was called-in by the Mayor of London and was overturned, but conditions were attached, including restrictions on windows overlooking the club and a requirement that all potential new residents are informed of the pre-existing use before they take occupancy.

Other approvals may also be necessary that relate directly to the site conditions. The timescale of these approvals and risk of delay should be evaluated as part of the Initial Project Brief. These regulations can include:

l building regulations (site conditions, spread of fire, access for the disabled)
l fire regulations (certain building types)
l party walls
l access rights
l road closures
l licence for work on Canals and Rivers Trust land
l Network Rail approval
l Civil Aviation Authority or Ministry of Defence restrictions.

Conducting pre-application discussions

The RIBA Plan of Work 2013 suggests that pre-application discussions should take place at Stage 1. The requirements for these meetings vary from authority to authority and so these should be checked before an appointment is booked. They can include pre-submission of:

l a draft proposed agenda
l confirmation of the level of officer
l suggested length of and venue for the meeting
l location plan identifying the site and its boundaries
l a description of the proposed development, including uses
l amount of development, numbers of dwellings or proposed floor space
l key building dimensions
l site constraints diagram
l fee for the meeting
l heritage statement.

Agenda for a pre-application meeting

- Introductions
- Description of proposed development
- Proposed programme
- Site constraints
- Planning history
  - ○ permitted development
  - ○ existing use
- Planning policy context
  - ○ national policy
  - ○ special national and local designations
  - ○ community engagement
  - ○ LPA's design requirements
- Statutory bodies that the LPA will consult (eg the highway authority, English Heritage)
- Validation requirements identified
- Requirement for an environmental impact assessment
- Community Infrastructure Levy
- Requirement for subsequent meetings
- Issue of meeting notes

Some LPAs' requirements are so detailed they can preclude early discussion with the LPA on the principle of the development. Other LPAs are difficult to engage in discussion at all. In such circumstances it may be necessary to make a 'tester application' and commence discussions on that basis. This can then be withdrawn once the planning parameters have been established. For major schemes, approaches at senior officer level or to the elected members of the council may be necessary to begin the dialogue and to establish the planning case for the proposal before major site investigation works are commenced. In some instances, for example large commercial projects with complex issues and numerous stakeholders, a planning performance agreement may be an appropriate vehicle.

Meeting notes

It is important to take notes at the meeting. Minutes may be provided by the planning officer after the meeting, but these will need to be cross-checked. Failure or refusal by an LPA to address issues relating to a proposal that is subsequently allowed at appeal can lead to costs being awarded against the LPA, which will go some way to reimbursing a client who has been forced to expend considerable amounts of money obtaining planning approval. However, it is important to note that advice given by officers at pre-application meetings is not binding on the LPA. The decision whether to approve the scheme or not is made by the planning committee or under delegated powers by senior officers. It is not unusual to have conflicting opinions between officers or for planning committees to make decisions against officers' advice. The agent needs to ensure that the client is aware of this risk and is kept aware of what advice the design team is working to. If the decision is different from this advice, the responsibility for the outcome is not the agent's; however, uninformed clients may believe that it is.

Planning performance agreements

Planning performance agreements (PPAs) create the framework for a collaborative process between the LPA, the developer and its agents, and key stakeholders, such as the highway authority, in developing, processing and determining a planning application.

The various parties work together from an early stage in a collaborative project management process, with the intention of creating greater certainty and transparency for the developer. The NPPF makes reference to PPAs at paragraph 195.

Paragraph 195 of the National Planning Policy Framework

Applicants and local planning authorities should consider the potential of entering into planning performance agreements, where this might achieve a faster and more effective application process.

Like all collaborative processes, PPAs require the enthusiastic cooperation of all parties and experience will inform the decision as to whether they are a suitable mechanism for a particular project and LPA.

Identifying validation requirements

A key outcome of the pre-application discussion will be an indication of what information will be required at the time that the application is made to enable the LPA to validate the application. The requirements come from a national list defined by statute and local lists devised by each authority.

National list

The information required to make a valid planning application consists of:

I Mandatory national information requirements specified in the General Permitted Development Order:
  o design and access statement, for large developments only (lower thresholds for conservation areas and World Heritage Sites)
  o location plan
  o site plan
  o ownership certificate
  o notices
  o agricultural holdings certificate
  o correct fee.
I Information provided on the standard application form.
I Information to accompany the application as specified by the LPA on its local list of information requirements.

(See pages 100–107: Stage 3 for details of these requirements.)

Local lists

Each LPA can require supporting information from a list that it specifies. These lists are frequently lengthy and certain requirements can have a significant impact on both the Project Programme and the Project Budget. Much of the information will require the appointment of specialist consultants and so consultants' fees should be accounted for in the Project Budget. A typical list is reproduced below with the possible impacts of each requirement. Requirements can be challenged using an Article 10(a) notice, which can be submitted either with an application or subsequent to validation being refused. If the LPA does not agree that the validation requirement is unnecessary the matter can be appealed to the Secretary of State (see page 114: Stage 3).

Table 1.1   Possible requirements for validation

INFORMATION REQUIRED	PROJECT ROLE	BUDGET IMPLICATIONS	PROGRAMME IMPLICATIONS	RISK
Air quality assessment	Environmental consultant	Fees	Survey and report preparation	Proposed use prevented or mitigation required
Affordable housing statement	Planning consultant	Reduced margins on development	Identify registered social landlord partner	Viability of the scheme
Arboricultural report	Arboriculturalist	Fees, costs of root protection	Survey and report preparation	Tree Preservation Orders constrain development area
Archaeological survey	Archaeologist	Initial fees, cost of excavation or watching brief	Pre-commencement excavation will delay construction start or progress of works	Budget and Programme
Biodiversity survey and report	Ecologist	Fees, cost of mitigation	Seasonal delays for surveys and start of construction	Frequent third party planning issue
Coal mining risk assessment	Coal Authority	Cost of foundations		Budget
Daylight/ sunlight assessment	Lighting consultant	Fees and mitigation		Higher performance standard
Drainage assessment	Civil engineer	Fees and mitigation, including sustainable drainage systems (SuDS) and off-mains foul drainage	Pre-commencement conditions may delay start. Off-site connections may cause delay	Budget and Programme
Economic statement	Planning Consultant	Fees		

Table 1.1   *Continued*

INFORMATION REQUIRED	PROJECT ROLE	BUDGET IMPLICATIONS	PROGRAMME IMPLICATIONS	RISK
Environmental impact assessment	Ecologist/civil engineer	Fees and any identified mitigation	Mitigation works	Budget and Programme
Financial viability statement	Planning consultant	Fees	Need to establish viability/non-viability. May include market testing over several years before planning submission	Programme
Flood risk assessment	Civil engineer	Fees. Off-site flood mitigation works could be costly	Mitigation works	Project may not be permitted in a flood zone or a limit of water displacement restricts ground print
Heritage assessment	Heritage consultant	Fees	High level of specification	Design implications
Highway safety statement	Highway engineer	Fees and costly off-site works	Pre-commencement works may delay site start	Budget and Programme
Land contamination assessment	Civil engineer	Fees and costly mitigation, which can include soil removal and decontamination	Pre-commencement mitigation works may delay start	Budget and Programme
Landscape and visual impact assessment	Landscape architect	Fees and any identified mitigation		Cost of any mitigation
Landscaping scheme	Landscape architect	Fees		
Lighting scheme	Lighting consultant	Fees		Cost of any mitigation

Table 1.1   Continued

INFORMATION REQUIRED	PROJECT ROLE	BUDGET IMPLICATIONS	PROGRAMME IMPLICATIONS	RISK
Noise and vibration assessment	Acoustic consultant	Fees and any identified mitigation		Proposed use prevented or mitigation required
Open space assessment	Planning consultant	Fees		Additional space requirement
Parking provision statement	Highway engineer	Fees		Additional space requirement
Photographs and photomontages	Various	Fees		
Planning statement	Planning consultant	Fees		
Planning obligations – draft heads of terms	Planning consultant	Fees, Community Infrastructure Levy costs	Legal delays	Project viability
Statement of community involvement	Planning consultant	Fees and costs of consultation		
Structural survey	Structural engineer	Fees and cost of remedial work		Structural instability
Transport assessment	Transport consultant	Fees		Scheme viability
Travel plan	Transport consultant	Fees		
Site waste management plan	Waste engineer	Fees and any identified mitigation		Cost of any mitigation

For requirements that can affect the viability of a project, it is advised that any risks to the project are identified early, by means of an assessment or survey at Stage 0 or Stage 1. Other matters can be left to be completed during Stage 2 without jeopardising the Project Programme; however, this must be assessed on a case-by-case basis. The planning strategy should identify the key assessments needed to reduce risk as early as Stage 0 (see page 40: Stage 0), particularly as the involvement of additional consultants has implications for the Project Execution Plan, Project Roles Table and the Schedule of Services and consequently for fees to be added to the Project Budget.

Domestic projects at Stage 1

Once the site has been identified for a domestic project, surveys of the site and any buildings will provide a clear indication of the potential for development and any constraints. They may also reveal that permitted development rights make a planning application unnecessary, although prior notification or neighbour consultations may be required. A lawful development certificate may be required to secure any use or development where the planning history is unclear.

A planning history, including establishing the existing use, will inform the planning advice provided to the client, who should be kept informed at all times on the progress of discussions with the planning authority. The client may also wish to attend any pre-application meetings that may take place at this stage. A realistic appraisal of the timescale for obtaining approval should be provided to the client as domestic clients frequently have little experience and high expectations of the process and may be disappointed or, worse, financially stretched by a lengthy planning process. The client should be advised of any additional information that may be required to support the application and given help in identifying suitably qualified specialists to carry out surveys.

Preparing Stage 1 Site Information and planning report

The output at this stage may be a report on the investigations to inform the Initial Project Brief.

Contents of Stage 1 Site Information and planning report

Site Information

- Constraints plan summarising survey results
- Topographical survey and commentary
- Measured building survey and commentary on any design constraints
- Summary of building conditions survey report, with implications for planning and listed building consent applications
- Risk analysis of constraints and identification of where further investigation is required
- Ground conditions report and recommendation of any further investigations required
- Environmental sensitivities
- Risks to the Project Programme and Project Budget.

Planning report

- The planning context for the site and project
- Permitted development opportunities
- Opportunities suggested by the planning history
- The case for betterment
- The policy environment and project compatibility
- Changes in the policy environment that will influence the planning case
- The consultant appointments necessary to complete the planning application
- Risks to the Project Programme and Project Budget, including a caution that outcomes at planning cannot be accurately predicted
- The planning strategy, and how it can meet the Project Objectives.

Chapter summary 1

At Stage 1 of the RIBA Plan of Work 2013 the key activities associated with town planning are the initial appraisal of the site and collation of the Site Information. Several Feasibility Studies may be undertaken to explore the implications of the opportunities and constraints identified before the Concept Design is developed at Stage 2. Subject to the client's requirements, this may entail detailed analysis of the planning context, including pre-application discussions with the planning authority.

It is possible that the validation requirements for the planning application will require the appointment of specialist consultants, who need to be included in the Information Exchange and factored into the Project Programme and Project Budget. This stage may also include making planning applications to establish the use of the site ahead of the preparation of detailed proposals.

The outcomes of the site investigations and the planning strategy are fed into the Initial Project Brief which is included in the Site Information and the Stage 1 planning report in the Stage 1 Information Exchange.

Concept Design

Chapter overview

The Concept Design is prepared at Stage 2 and this output can be used to make a detailed planning application if required by the planning strategy. However, as this stage requires only outline proposals for the architectural, structural and building services design, there is a high risk of subsequent changes that could affect the approved scheme. This chapter discusses these risks and the benefits of collaboration with the planning authority and other parties as the design develops.

The key coverage in this chapter is as follows:

Taking the design forward with planning officers

Using design review

Consulting with other agencies

Community liaison

Coordinating consultants' submissions

Developing the design and access statement

Planning in the Stage 2 report

Making planning applications based on Stage 2 outputs.

Introduction

The preparation of the Concept Design requires collaboration with fellow members of the design team as well as with any consultants providing the supporting information for the planning application, as identified in chapter 1. As knowledge and understanding of the constraints and opportunities for the project increase and as the design develops, it is helpful to establish a dialogue with the planning authority to allow its officers to make informed comments on the proposals before the application is submitted. For sensitive schemes, due to their size or their location, it may be advisable to have the early design proposals assessed at design review. For some local authorities this is now a validation requirement and for some schemes this may involve several sessions as the design develops. This should be allowed for in the Design Programme.

The site investigation may have identified particular issues that necessitate consultation with other agencies, such as the highway authority or English Heritage. If they are amenable it is helpful to receive their contributions to the design development before they are consulted as part of the application process to ensure that their concerns are addressed. This will help to reduce the number of changes required when further design work has been undertaken.

For larger proposals a thorough process of community liaison should begin at this stage, with commentary from people and businesses that may be affected by the proposal.

It is important that the information gathered from specialist consultants is coordinated by the lead designer and that it all informs and supports the design proposal. On large projects there will be a considerable number of reports; any conflicting evidence will make the application process more difficult and could be taken up by objectors to support their cause. The agent or project lead making the application will need to be fully aware of the content of all of the gathered evidence to be able to undertake informed negotiations with the planning authority. Major projects require a design and access statement; it is helpful at this stage to make this a working document available to the client and the design team as an update which includes the design development and a summary of the constraints. It should also be accompanied by an appraisal of the implications of any changes to the scheme required for planning on the Project Budget and Project Programme.

If an application is to be made based on the outputs from Stage 2, the client must be appraised of the risks and appropriate contingencies identified to mitigate the potential delay involved in seeking further planning permission should changes subsequently prove to be necessary.

What are the Core Objectives of this stage?

The Core Objectives of the RIBA Plan of Work 2013 at Stage 2 are:

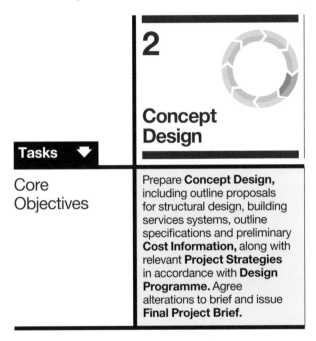

The Concept Design, which integrates the outline proposals of the design team, should be developed through an iterative process of dialogue with the planning authority, so that the likely cost and programme implications along with design planning requirements are reflected in the Final Project Brief.

Taking the design forward with planning officers

A successful outcome to a planning application will often be the result of close collaboration with the planning officers before the application is made. If possible, pre-application discussions should be commenced at Stage 1 (see page 67: Stage 1), and provided that the planning authority is amenable and the client is prepared to pay the fees that may be charged for each meeting, these should be continued throughout Stage 2. In instances of best practice this is an iterative process in which the constraints and the design response are reviewed as the design develops. It is helpful if relevant parties such as the highway authority and conservation officers are party to these discussions. Similarly, if particular issues are identified it may be helpful to have the specialist consultants (eg highway engineer, ecologist or landscape architect) attend at least one meeting so that the issues can be discussed and actions agreed between the design team and the planning authority. It should always be borne in mind that the advice given is not binding on the authority and that the decision on the application is made either by senior officers or by the planning committee.

Using design review

For schemes in sensitive locations and for all major development proposals it can be advisable, or even necessary, to submit the scheme for design review.

Design review

Design review is an independent and impartial evaluation process in which a panel of experts on the built environment assesses the design of a proposal. Projects subjected to a design review are usually of public significance, and the process is designed to improve the quality of buildings and places for the benefit of the public.

Some local authorities are now making this a validation requirement for some projects. Design review is supported by the NPPF, which states:

Paragraph 62 of the National Planning Policy Framework

Local planning authorities should have local design review arrangements in place to provide assessment and support to ensure high standards of design. They should also when appropriate refer major projects for a national design review. In general, early engagement on design produces the greatest benefits. In assessing applications, local planning authorities should have regard to the recommendations from the design review panel.

Design review is offered by a number of agencies, including in-house teams within planning authorities and local voluntary panels. The Design Network, supported by the Design Council, the RIBA, the Royal Town Planning Institute (RTPI) and the Landscape Institute, offers a regional service. It is usual to find a service proportionate to the scheme under discussion. Design reviews may be instigated after a request from the planning authority, or they may be requested by the applicant to support more innovative and aspirational schemes.

Design Review: Principles and Practice

The RIBA with the Landscape Institute and RTPI worked with the Design Council and CABE (the Commission for Architecture and the Built Environment, now part of the Design Council) to produce guidance on the use of design review in *Design Review: Principles and Practice*.

Design review:

- is conducted by expert practitioners with current experience in design and development, a record of good design in their own projects and the skills to appraise schemes objectively
- offers feedback and observations that will lead to the improvement of schemes, but does not redesign them
- gives decision makers the confidence and information to support innovative, high-quality designs that meet the needs of their communities and customers, and to resist poorly designed schemes.

Design is a subjective, sometimes emotive issue. It is important to the success of the scheme that the outcome of the design review process is a report setting out the findings in planning terms, to enable the decision makers to make an informed planning-led decision on design.

Consulting with other agencies

Physical site constraints can have significant impacts on the design of a scheme and chapter 1 sets out how these can be identified. In order to develop a scheme that is likely to succeed at planning, a dialogue with the relevant agencies is appropriate at Stage 2 – if they are willing to engage. The RIBA Plan of Work 2013 identifies these agencies generically as third parties, but this term is usually reserved for those making non-professional representations at application or appeal stage. The agencies will be consulted as part of the application process, but their responses are often received late in the determination period and consequently can be difficult to respond to without agreeing to extend the determination period, or even by withdrawing the application. Early understanding of their requirements is therefore important. The National Planning Policy Framework states:

Paragraph 192 of the National Planning Policy Framework

The right information is crucial to good decision-taking, particularly where formal assessments are required (such as Environmental Impact Assessment, Habitats Regulations Assessment and Flood Risk Assessment). To avoid delay, applicants should discuss what information is needed with the local planning authority and expert bodies as early as possible.

The agencies can include:

I Canals and Rivers Trust
I Civil Aviation Authority
I Coal Authority
I Environment Agency
I English Heritage

I   Health and Safety Executive
I   Highways Agency
I   highway authorities
I   Natural England
I   Network Rail
I   Sport England.

The planning authority may also consult other agencies; it is advisable to approach these at an early stage as well, if relevant:

I   conservation area advisory committees
I   county archaeological officers
I   drainage board
I   emergency services and multi-agency emergency planning
I   health authorities and agencies
I   local authority environmental health officers
I   navigation authorities
I   police architectural liaison officers and crime prevention design advisers
I   schools and colleges
I   waste disposal authorities
I   water and sewerage undertakers.

Community liaison

For major projects it will be necessary to submit a statement of community engagement. The nature of the consultation process and the identification of stakeholders will be proportionate and relevant to the proposal, but can include local residents, interest groups and businesses. The process may involve distributing leaflets to canvass opinion, holding an exhibition at which to gather comments or holding a workshop to incorporate community aspirations into the proposal. The RTPI has published guidance on effective engagement in its *Good Practice Guide to Public Engagement in Development Schemes*.

The degree of community engagement will vary with each scheme; however, even small domestic proposals may prompt fewer objections to the final application if neighbours have been consulted in a positive and responsive way.

Coordinating consultants' submissions

An important role for the project lead or the planning consultant coordinating the planning application will be to ensure that all of the reports and surveys support the application as finally presented and, if necessary, are reviewed in the light of design changes. Inconsistencies will undermine the application and any subsequent appeal. For example, it is important to check the consistency of:

I tree root protection with ground-works and drainage proposals
I landscape schemes with ecology reports
I noise and vibration mitigation with landscape proposals
I archaeologists' reports with heritage assessments.

Developing the design and access statement

The Planning Portal gives the following guidance:

Design and access statements

A design and access statement (DAS) is a short report accompanying and supporting a planning application. It will provide a framework for applicants to explain how a proposed development is a suitable response to the site and its setting, and demonstrate that it can be adequately accessed by prospective users.

A DAS is required with planning applications for major development – both full and outline. Lower thresholds apply in conservation areas and World Heritage Sites, where some smaller applications must also be accompanied by a DAS. Listed building consent applications must also include a DAS. Applications for waste development, a material change of use, engineering or mining operations do not need to be accompanied by a DAS.

A DAS must explain the design principles and concepts that have been applied to the development. It must also demonstrate how the proposed development's context has influenced the design. The DAS must explain the applicant's approach to access and how relevant local plan policies have been taken into account, any consultation undertaken in relation to access issues, and how the outcome of this consultation has informed the proposed development. Applicants must also explain how any specific issues which might affect access to the proposed development have been addressed.

The level of detail in a DAS should be proportionate to the complexity of the application, but it should not be long. For most straightforward planning applications, the DAS may only need to be a page long.

As the Planning Portal implies, there has been a tendency to make the design and access statements overlong. However, they can be a useful tool during the design stage, as a vehicle for communicating to the design team the information that is informing the design development. The CABE publication *Design and Access Statements: How to Write, Read and Use Them*, while supporting a more lengthy and discursive document, also encourages their use for guiding the design process.

In practice, consultants derive their own headings relevant to the sector and scale of their submissions. It is helpful to use a standard practice framework for the final statement to ensure that all constraints have been considered during the design process and are properly summarised.

Planning in the Stage 2 report

The Stage 2 planning report produced by the lead designer or the planning consultant should:

I set out progress in planning matters against the planning strategy defined in the previous stages

I identify any additional constraints and opportunities identified through the surveys and consultations

I identify any additional consultancy required for validation

I comment on the approach that the planning authority is taking towards the proposed scheme

I comment on any implications for the Project Programme and the Project Budget that have arisen as the design has developed, including contingencies for reapplication for non-material changes.

The Final Project Brief is an output at the end of Stage 2 and will contain the items scheduled above.

The Construction Strategy is set out at Stage 2 and ideally should contain the requirements to satisfy construction stage conditions. If these can be predicted they should be included now to avoid adjustments after planning approval is granted and the conditions known. Typically these will be operational issues, such as noise and dust control.

Making planning applications based on Stage 2 outputs

Clients may wish to minimise their spending on design fees until the risks associated with obtaining planning approval have been resolved. This can be achieved by making the detailed planning application on the basis of the Stage 2 outputs, which can be based on minimal contributions from the design team. However, while some reports and surveys will be necessary for validation of the application, alone they may not provide a complete picture of the site and the context for the application.

The project lead and lead designer should be aware of the professional risks of making design decisions based on incomplete information and ensure that they have the competence and experience to make the necessary judgments. Where there is clearly a risk, for example ground conditions that may not be favourable in part of the site, the project lead should communicate the risk to the client together with the possible implications if a subsequent survey were to show that conditions necessitate a redesign and reapplication. The architect should make clear what risks they are not covering.

Structural and services engineering inputs can have a significant impact on the overall shape and appearance of a building, for example plant rooms at roof level and structural zones affecting floor-to-floor heights. If the planning approval is gained without these elements being considered and they are subsequently required for a functioning building, an application will be needed for material or non-material amendment to the scheme (see page 144: Stage 5), which creates risk of additional cost and delay. The constructed building has to be in accordance with the approved plans; if it is not, it is deemed that the consent no longer exists. There is no definition of non-material amendment and it is defined on a case-by-case basis, which clearly introduces risk. If the amendment is deemed to be material, a full application will have to be made again for the scheme, with all the attendant cost and delay.

The client should also be made aware of the implications of any changes it might wish to make to the brief after the end of Stage 2, particularly if the concept design is used for the planning application. In such instances the Stage 2 sign-off should be very clear in stating the risks of client's design changes to the status of the planning approval.

Domestic projects at Stage 2

Pre-application meetings for domestic projects usually take place at this stage, when the client's design requirements have been defined and the Concept Design represents their aspirations for the project. The client should be made aware of the possibility of design changes as a result of this consultation and again they may wish to attend the pre-application meetings. It is important to make notes of the meetings and record how and why the design has developed because, although design and access statements are not required for minor and householder applications, being able to recall the reasons for design changes may be useful in deterring the client from requesting changes after planning consent has been obtained.

Chapter summary 2

The keys to developing a successful planning application are communication and consultation. Stage 2 is the part of the project in which reaching the right people – those who can agree effective strategies to design for the opportunities and constraints that the project presents – is vital to a successful outcome. Working effectively with the local planning authority, statutory bodies, the community and the other consultants and design team members will greatly reduce the risk of failure at the decision stage.

The RIBA recommends that detailed planning applications are made on the basis of Stage 3 outputs. However, in some circumstances and for some clients, applications are made at the end of Stage 2. This should only be done if the design team and the client fully recognise the risks that this carries.

Developed Design

Chapter overview

The RIBA Plan of Work 2013 recommends that applications for detailed planning permission are made with the Stage 3 output. This output is a fully coordinated response from the core designers and the basic spatial parameters are unlikely to be changed as the Technical Design is progressed in the next stage (Stage 4). The Cost Information will be aligned to the Project Budget. It can therefore be confidently presented in a planning application as the design that will be constructed without major amendment.

The RIBA Plan of Work 2013 also recommends that the Technical Design does not commence until planning permission is obtained.

This chapter sets out the application process and the client's options if planning permission is refused.

The key coverage in this chapter is as follows:

Making the application

Identifying the appropriate form of consent to be applied for

Preparing drawings and BIM models for planning purposes

Preparing other supporting documentation, fees and certificates

Obtaining validation for an application

Supporting the decision-making process

The determination period

Consultation

Progress of the application

Preparing section 106 agreements

The officer's assessment

Making representations at planning committees

The decision – approval and options on refusal

Making an appeal

Forms of appeal

Appeals and the Project Programme and Project Budget

Introduction

This chapter is in three sections:

Making the application

Supporting the decision-making process

Making an appeal

The application is the culmination of the preparatory work from the preceding stages supporting the Developed Design. The actions in terms of planning are largely procedural and this chapter sets out how to meet the requirements of the process. Additional support at key points during the decision-making process can assist the scheme to achieve a successful determination and suggestions for this are set out in the second part of the chapter. Finally, if the application is unsuccessful, the strategies and processes for appealing the decision are given. The time frames of the appeals process and the possible implications of delays within it are set out. If it becomes necessary to appeal, target timescales are given; however, these are subject to the availability of the parties, including the Planning Inspectorate.

What are the Core Objectives of this stage?

The Core Objectives of the RIBA Plan of Work 2013 at Stage 3 are:

3

Developed Design

Tasks ▼

Core Objectives

Prepare **Developed Design**, including coordinated and updated proposals for structural design, building services systems, outline specifications, **Cost Information** and **Project Strategies** in accordance with **Design Programme**.

The RIBA advises that the planning application is made based on the Information Exchanges from Stage 3, when the Developed Design contains the coordinated proposals from other design team members and represents the scheme that will be built without material amendments that would affect the planning consent. The Project Programme may be affected by delays in the planning process at this stage.

Making the application

Making the application is a process of assembling the scheme details and supporting information that have been prepared during the earlier Plan of Work stages and submitting them with the appropriate forms, fees and ownership details.

Identifying the appropriate form of consent to be applied for

If it is not already clear from the planning strategy, the type of planning application to be made will need to be defined and the appropriate application form and process selected. The types of application (including those already mentioned in for earlier stages) are as follows:

Applications for planning consent

I Full consent for operational development (major)
I Full consent for operational development (minor)
I Change of use
I Householder development
I Advertisement
I Outline application (see page 61: Stage 1)
I Reserved matters
I Hybrid applications (part full, part outline)
I Removal or variation of conditions (see page 128: Stage 4)
I Approval of conditions (see page 143: Stage 5)
I Consents under Tree Preservation Orders
I Extending the time limit of an existing consent
I Non-material amendments

Applications for certificates

I Lawful development certificate (see page 62: Stage 1)
I Certificate of lawfulness of existing use or development (CLEUD) (see page 63: Stage 1)
I Prior notification for forestry, agriculture (including new permitted development rights for barn conversions), demolition, telecommunications

Other consents under the Planning (Listed Building and Conservation Areas) Act 1990

I   Listed building consent
I   Conservation area consent
I   Notification of proposed works to trees in conservation areas

Planning forms

Most, but not all, of the application forms are available online through the Planning Portal, which also gives guidance notes on the use of each.

www.planningportal.gov.uk/planning/applications/howtoapply/permissiontypes

Preparing drawings and BIM models for planning purposes

The national validation list requires that all applications be accompanied by a location plan and a site plan. The local planning authority (LPA) will also require drawings to adequately describe the scheme which, for buildings for which full permission is sought, are likely to include those listed in table 3.1.

BIM (Building Information Modelling) models are not yet accepted as part of planning applications; however, they can generate drawings to an appropriate scale and with the necessary information to be submitted as an output at Stage 3. A BIM model also has the advantage that its outputs are fully coordinated, something that can be difficult to achieve with 2D drawings.

The drawings submitted for planning consent are to be read by lay members of the local authority and the general public, therefore 3D images and street elevations – which are not necessarily part of the requirements for validation – can be of great value in helping people to understand the proposal. Good visual images are significant elements of added value that a qualified and experienced project team can bring to the project.

Table 3.1   Requirements for planning drawings

DRAWING	SCALE	SCALE BAR	REQUIREMENT	REQUIREMENT	REQUIREMENT	REQUIREMENT	REQUIREMENT
Location plan	1:2500/1:1250	Yes	Red line: application area	Blue line: other land in applicant's ownership	OS licence number		Distances of buildings from boundaries
Site plan	1:500/1:200	Yes	Red line: application area	Blue line: other land in applicant's ownership	North sign	Boundaries and boundary treatment	
			Trees: location, girth, spread, root protection area	Levels	Key to surface treatment	Drainage	45 degree splays from residential windows
Floor plans, existing and proposed	1:200/1:100/1:50	Yes	Clear labelling	Levels			
Elevations, existing and proposed	1:200/1:100/1:50	Yes	Clear labelling	Small key plan to identify elevations	Materials		
Sections through site	1:200/1:100/1:50	Yes	Clear labelling	Small key plan to identify sections	Heights and levels	Through site and adjacent development	

The Stage 3 Information Exchanges also go to the design team for the Technical Design stage. If the planning process leads to changes to the design, these changes have to be communicated to all.

Copyright

The copyright for the drawings and the design resides either with the designer or, if agreed by licence or occasionally in the appointment, with the client. The dissemination of digital images through the planning process lays this open to abuse. Designers can define their intellectual property rights by an appropriate note on each drawing and by formatting the plans as PDF files, which makes them less accessible for transfer to other sites and projects.

Planning permission goes with the land. This means that if the client sells the site on with the benefit of permission there is a risk that the new owner may use designs without the designer's agreement. It is therefore advisable that the designer's appointment contains a clause defining their intellectual property rights, reducing the risk of abuse of their information by others.

RIBA Concise Conditions of Appointment 2010 (2012 Revision) – cause 6.1 (in part): copyright and use of information

The Architect shall own all intellectual property rights including the copyright in the drawings and documents produced in performing the Services and generally asserts the Architect's moral rights to be identified as the author of such work.

And

The Architect shall not be liable for any use of the drawings and documents other than for the purpose for which they were prepared.

Preparing other supporting documentation, fees and certificates

The application will be accompanied by the appropriate forms identified above and the documentation that has been identified as necessary to validate the application (see table 1.1, page 71). Other documents, for example a planning statement, may not have been required by the LPA for validation and can follow shortly afterwards; however, it is advisable to make a full submission to be viewed as a complete case by the planning officers, elected members and interested third parties. Where the client's resources permit it is also advisable to submit as much detail as possible to reduce the number of conditions and increase certainty as the project enters Stage 4.

Supporting documentation

During the development of the scheme, the supporting Site Information will have been assembled and coordinated by the project lead, who will also have identified what further surveys and reports are likely to be conditioned on an approval. For example, if a contaminated land desktop, tier 1 study has identified the presence of contaminants on the site, any approval is likely to require a tier 2 study and full specification of remedial work as a pre-commencement condition.

Fees

The planning authority is entitled to charge a fee for applications. The exceptions to this include repeat submissions made within 12 months of the original application, applications for disabled facilities supported by relevant documentation and applications for conservation area and listed building consents.

Planning fees

Guidance on the fees for planning applications in England is provided at:

www.planningportal.gov.uk/uploads/english_application_fees.pdf

A fees calculator is also provided on the online forms.

Some authorities will accept electronic payments, others require a cheque. Where this money is handled through the agent's practice it should be held in the client's account until submitted with the application. Alternatively, the client can arrange to pay the fee directly to the local authority.

Land ownership and tenancy certificates

For every application the land ownership and interests need to be identified, and if the application area defined by the red line on the plan is not entirely within the ownership and control of the applicant, notices must be served on the other owners. The application must be accompanied by a correctly completed section 12 certificate.

The term 'owner' means a person having a freehold interest or a leasehold interest, the unexpired term of which is not less than seven years. It is possible for a site to have several 'owners' under this definition. It is essential that these certificates are correct because the application is invalid if they are not.

Checking current land ownership

Clients do not always advise their agents of changes in ownership and it essential to check this information for every application at all stages – full or outline – and for reserved matters and conditions applications and, if necessary, on submitting an appeal.

I Certificate A is completed if the applicant is the only owner of all the land within the boundaries of the application site. If the applicant is not the only owner then one of the following alternative certificates must be completed.
I Certificate B is completed if the applicant knows the names and addresses of all the owners of the land involved in the application.
I Certificate C is completed if the applicant knows the names and addresses of some, but not all, of the owners of the land involved in the application.
I Certificate D is completed if the applicant does not know the names and addresses of any of the owners of the land involved in the application.

Where the owners are known, including those identified on certificate C, a Notice 1 is served on them. This is reproduced below.

Town and Country Planning (Development Management Procedure) (England) Order 2010 NOTICE UNDER ARTICLE 11 OF APPLICATION FOR PLANNING PERMISSION

(Notice 1: This notice is to be printed and served on individuals if Certificate B or C is completed)

Proposed development at:

Name or flat number

Property number or name

Street

Locality

Town

County

Postal town

Postcode

Take notice that application is being made by:

Organisation name

Applicant name   Title   Forename

Surname

For planning permission to:

Description of proposed development

Local Planning Authority to whom the application is being submitted:

Local Planning Authority address:

Any owner of the land or tenant who wishes to make representations about this application, should write to the council within 21 days of the date of this notice.

Signatory:

Signatory   Title   Forename

Surname

Signature

Date (dd-mm-yyyy)

Statement of owners' rights: The grant of planning permission does not affect owners' rights to retain or dispose of their property, unless there is some provision to the contrary in an agreement or lease.

Statement of agricultural tenants' rights: The grant of planning permission for non-agricultural development may affect agricultural tenants' security of tenure.

'Owner' means a person having a freehold interest or a leasehold interest the unexpired term of which is not less than seven years.
'Tenant' means a tenant of an agricultural holding any part of which is comprised in the land.

Once completed this form needs to be served on the owner(s) or tenant(s)

Where the owners are not known, either under certificate C or D, a Notice 2 is submitted for publication by a local newspaper and also submitted to the planning authority with the application. The notices give details of the application and where the plans can be viewed.

The certificates form part of the application form and the notices can be downloaded from the Planning Portal.

The land ownership certificates also include the agricultural holdings certificate, which must be completed even if the project does not involve an agricultural use or agricultural land. If agricultural tenants are affected by the proposal they must be notified of the application.

Obtaining validation for an application

Applications are generally made electronically via the Planning Portal. Local authorities vary in the degree to which they can handle electronic information, so this should be established first. Once received, the applications are checked by a clerk and, if considered complete, a letter is issued confirming that the application is being considered. Validation in itself does not confirm the acceptability of any of the contents of the application and is merely procedural.

The time taken to validate applications can vary depending on the resources available within the authority; local experience will inform the evaluation of potential delay to the Project Programme. To minimise the risk of delays at validation, pre-application discussions should cover the likely requirements. Local knowledge will also aid understanding the particular presentational requirements for drawn information for the LPA, although this can vary from one officer to another.

As mentioned for Stage 1, if additional and possibly unforeseen information is requested in order to validate the application, this can be challenged using an Article 10(a) notice, either submitted with an application or subsequent to validation being refused. If the LPA does not agree that the validation requirement is unnecessary the matter can be appealed to the Secretary of State (see page 114: Stage 3).

Domestic projects at Stage 3

Applications

Many minor domestic planning applications can be made on the householder application form, which requires much less information. The Planning Portal has details at:

www.planningportal.gov.uk/permission/

To reduce the need to make applications for material and non-material changes later in the project, planning applications for full planning permission should be made with the Developed Design at Stage 3. The chances of success and a speedier decision are increased if the detail submitted is a full as possible and based on the issues raised at the pre-application discussions. Clients should be made aware of the delays that might occur that are beyond the control of the design team throughout the application process.

Supporting the decision-making process

It is important to be aware of how the decision-making process operates and when it will be helpful to contact the LPA during the determination period to ensure that it has all the information required or where amendments to the proposal are likely to make it more acceptable. Contact with the officers dealing with the application will alert the agent to any issues and give the team an opportunity to respond in a timely way to improve the chances of success.

The determination period

Once it has been confirmed that the application contains the necessary information for validation the planning authority commences the determination period. Legally, the period begins on the date that the complete application is submitted, not when it is validated, which is significant when considering appeals for non-determination. Generally, however, LPAs define the start of the determination period as the date of the validation letter.

Determination period

The time defined as the target period for planning authorities to reach and publish a decision on a planning application.

The target time requirements for the planning process are set out by the Secretary of State. The target decision periods for applications for outline, reserved matters and conditions are eight weeks for minor applications and 13 weeks for major applications.

A major application can be defined as any of the following:

I residential development of 10 or more homes
I residential development on a site of at least 0.5 hectares
I non-residential development on a site of at least 1 hectare
I creation or change of use of a commercial development, where the floor space is 1,000 square metres or more.

The LPA's performance is determined by the time taken to determine decisions and this may influence their approach to an application. It can result in delays in validating applications, which will have implications for the process of the application.

Where the LPA is concerned about meeting target dates and the target determination date is approaching, it may ask for an extension of time to consider information submitted during the application period, or alternatively it can refuse the application in anticipation that a revised submission will follow. Other authorities will let the application run on for an indefinite period.

Once the target determination date has been reached it is possible to appeal for non-determination. This option expires six months after the target determination date.

The project lead needs to be mindful of the potential for delay before, during and after the application process. As a starting point for programming, the project lead should make the client aware of this uncertainty in the programme and of their lack of control over the LPA's performance.

Consultation

The first action by the LPA is to put the application out to consultation. The parties approached can vary and may consist of statutory consultees, other interest groups and immediate neighbours. Some applications must be advertised in the local press. The agencies that may be consulted are listed on page 86 (Stage 2). Consultees are given 21 days to respond.

Progress of the application

Immediately after the 21-day period has ended it is advisable for the agent to contact the case officer to determine:

I what issues have been raised
I what further information is required
I how any harm that has been identified can be mitigated.

Many successful applications involve a degree of negotiation at this stage of the determination period. The lead designer should make the client and the project lead aware that design changes may arise from this and that they will need to be put through the Change Control Procedures, which start at this stage. Making changes may extend the determination period, with consequent impacts on the programme. These risks can be reduced, but possibly not eliminated, by effective pre-application consultation with the LPA and the relevant agencies.

From this point until the case officer has completed their report it is advisable to remain in contact with the LPA to track the progress of the application, to supply any further information and to obtain advance warning if a refusal is being recommended. All conversations and meetings should be recorded in writing and all email and letter correspondence retained in case an appeal is lodged and the issues covered become material to that appeal.

Preparing section 106 agreements

An agreement under section 106 of the Town and Country Planning Act 1990 can be used to make an otherwise unacceptable proposal acceptable to the LPA. The usual areas covered by these agreements are set out on page 37 (Stage 0). They can be drafted by the LPA or by agents for the applicant who have the requisite legal knowledge and experience of this area of the law. Planning approvals are frequently conditioned to require receipt of an agreed and signed undertaking before the decision notice is released. It is helpful at application stage to submit a draft agreement with the application, particularly if it is central to the success of the project, for example the provision of affordable housing.

Example of the use of a section 106 agreement

A large detached town house had been converted to use as a nursing home, with the rear garden used as parking for staff and visitors. Subsequently, the house had been reverted to a single dwelling house and sold on. An application was then made for planning permission for four houses on the garden. The LPA felt that the development would be acceptable only if the original house did not revert to nursing home use and so required a unilateral undertaking under section 106 by the developer and, by covenant, future owners of the house to prevent this from happening.

The officer's assessment

The case officer prepares a report that contains the following:

I Details of the scheme: description of proposal, applicant, agent, site address, end date of determination period
I Summary of representations received from third parties
I Site description
I Planning history
I Description of proposal
I Consultations
I Relevant policies
I Planning considerations: issues, material considerations and any harm identified
I Balancing exercise, conclusion and recommendation
I Suggested conditions

See pages 22–23 (Stage 0) for how planning decisions are made based on policy and on an assessment of harm and any material considerations for and against the proposal. The case officer's report then goes forward for decision by either the senior officers under delegated powers or by the planning committee. Which route is chosen is determined by the LPA's standing orders, which typically refer applications to the planning committee based on their size, impact, number of objections or at the request of a ward councillor.

Making representations at planning committees

The outcome of a committee decision is less predictable than one under delegated powers, when the consultations will have signposted the likely decision. Planning is a democratic process and local democracy can be influenced by factors other than planning law. Individual members can be influenced by lobbying by third parties for or against the proposal, and eloquent advocacy in the planning committee meeting can sway opinions on the day. Certain types of application have a very low success rate, with or without officer recommendation, because the elected members represent the opposition of the local residents to the nature of the development. Gypsy and traveller applications are one instance of this. In such cases it is as well to advise the client of the likelihood of a refusal and to be prepared to go to appeal. Generally, however, if it is becoming apparent that political opposition to the proposal is an issue, the client is able to lobby elected members for support for the proposal, in the same way as those who oppose the scheme will approach committee members to oppose it.

The planning officers should advise the agent if there will be an opportunity to speak at the committee and in almost all cases it is advisable to take this up. A set time will be allowed for speakers to put their cases, usually two or three minutes, and the committee members may put questions to the speakers after their presentations. It is important to make notes of the discussion and the vote for reference in any appeal or resubmission.

Speaking at planning committees

It is advisable to prepare a short speech and time its delivery in advance of the meeting. The case officer should be able to advise what drawings will be on display to illustrate the proposal and so reference can be made to them in the presentation.

Domestic projects at Stage 3

Determination period

During the process of the application contact should be made with the case officer after the 21-day consultation period and contact maintained until the decision notice is issued. This will provide opportunities to deal with any issues arising from the consultations or advance warning of the likely decision and how it will be determined. The client should be kept informed throughout this process and advised of any changes to the scheme or delays to the programme that are occurring.

The decision – approval

The content of a decision notice is set out on page 125 (Stage 4). If the scheme is approved, the project can move on to Stage 4: Technical Design.

The decision – options on refusal

If the application is refused, the project team should advise the client on the next steps. The options are:

I resubmit with amendments
I appeal the decision
I rethink or even abandon the scheme.

The decision notice will contain the reasons for refusal.

Understanding reasons for refusal

The reasons should fall into one of the following categories:

– A relatively minor issue has been raised that could be overcome but the principle of the development has been accepted by the LPA, suggesting that the scheme could be revised and resubmitted.

Understanding reasons for refusal (*continued*)

– The application has been refused on essentially political grounds but another decision maker could reach a more favourable conclusion, suggesting that it could be appealed.
– The application has been refused on local plan policies that conflict with national policy, suggesting that it could be appealed.
– The project has been refused on subjective grounds (usually design) but another decision maker could reach a more favourable conclusion, suggesting that it could be appealed.
– The project is fundamentally flawed in that it cannot meet policy requirements, both national and local, and any material considerations fall far short of overcoming any harm, suggesting the need for a radical rethink.

An experienced agent will be able to assess the chances of success at appeal and advise accordingly.

In some circumstances, particularly in appealing for non-determination, it may be advisable to twin-track the appeal; that is, to submit a duplicate application to the LPA, which gives it the opportunity to determine the application and avoid the cost of an appeal.

Making an appeal

There are options to appeal not only the decisions reached by local authorities, but also some perceived failures of process.

Information on making an appeal

Each type of application has a separate appeal procedure. The relevant forms can be found on the Planning Portal at:

www.planningportal.gov.uk/planning/appeals/online/makeanappeal

Appeals can be made against:

I   non-validation
I   non-determination
I   decision made by an LPA on a planning application
I   decision made by an LPA on a lawful development certificate
I   conditions
I   enforcement.

There are separate forms for:

I   householders
I   advertisements
I   conservation areas and listed buildings consent
I   conservation areas and listed buildings enforcement.

Forms of appeal

Appeals are heard by the Planning Inspectorate in one of three ways:

I   written representation
I   informal hearing
I   public inquiry.

The appellant can request the manner in which the case is heard; however, the Planning Inspectorate, known by the acronym PINS, will have the final say based on the amount of evidence to be reviewed, the case for public representation and the number of people attending. For appeals against planning decisions and non-determination, the procedures are as follows.

Written representation

The appeal form is accompanied by a statement from the appellant and supporting documentation that consists of the documents submitted with the planning application (or subsequent amendments that the decision was made on) and may also include further evidence that overcomes one or more reasons for refusal (eg a bat survey to support an application for a barn conversion not requested during the determination of the application). The LPA submits its response to this together with any third party representations. The paperwork is then sent to an inspector, who makes a site visit and writes up the decision letter. The site visit may be unaccompanied if the site and the impact of the proposal can be adequately considered from public viewpoints, otherwise the inspector will be required to enter the site and should be accompanied by representatives of the appellant and the LPA. No representations about the case can be made at the visit, but the inspector may ask for clarification of the location of the proposal and key views referred to in the evidence.

This type of appeal is suitable for most householder cases and minor applications where there has been limited third party representation, if it is not of a highly technical nature and further discussion of the merits of the case and the objections are not necessary to enable the inspector to reach their decision.

Informal hearing

The submission is similar to the written representation procedure. The appeal is conducted as an informal discussion chaired by the inspector, who makes an unaccompanied site visit just before the hearing and an accompanied one at the end of the hearing before it is closed. The discussion may include representatives from the appellant who, as well as their agent and local supporters, may be experts, to address particular areas, for example highways or landscape appraisal. The LPA may also have representatives who can address the issues from an expert stance, and there may also be representatives of third parties, often organised as protest groups or from the parish council.

Informal hearings are usually scheduled to last for one day, including the accompanied site visit. This can be a challenging timetable if there are a number of speakers and issues to address and hearings can be adjourned for a second day, so any fee proposal should reflect this possibility. The intention is to assist the inspector in reaching their decision and to add to and clarify the written submission, and they should chair the meeting to that agenda. If it becomes apparent before the appeal is heard that the number of issues or speakers makes this timetable impossible, there should be a discussion with PINS about extending to a second day or converting to a public inquiry.

Public inquiries

Public inquiries can be held over several days, or even weeks, depending on the size of the project and its complexity. They are scheduled when the nature of the project demands a public examination of the issues and its context; these can include highly technical matters, considerable public opposition or the legal interests of the appellants which extend beyond planning law. It is usual for the appellant, the LPA and any third party groups to engage barristers as advocates to conduct the case for their party. The proceedings are formal and can be taken under oath. The witnesses give their evidence seated and are first examined by the advocate from the side that appointed them, then cross-examined by the opposing party's advocate and then re-examined by their advocate to clarify any matters raised under the cross-examination. The inspector may also ask the witnesses to clarify certain points. The intention is to assist the inspector in reaching their decision, although the conduct is quasi-legalistic and often aggressive. Cross-examination can be designed to undermine the case for the opposing side as much as it is to draw out the facts of the case for the inspector.

Being a professional witness at a public inquiry

Being a witness at a public inquiry is challenging. Witnesses should give their considered professional opinion on issues on which they have expert knowledge and on nothing else. Acknowledging that there are areas that are subjective or that are beyond their expertise is helpful to the inspector in giving weight to the rest of their evidence and is not a sign of weakness on the part of the witness.

For appeals against enforcement, once the appeal notice is submitted, PINS sets the timetable and then submissions are made. This enables a rapid response to an enforcement notice, so that the appellant is not disadvantaged by having insufficient time to prepare their statement and proofs of evidence. See page 160 (Stage 7) for details on planning enforcement.

Appeals and the Project Programme and Project Budget

The decision to go to appeal should be made after consideration of the impact on the Project Programme and on the Project Budget. In most cases, an appeal will only be made when no other avenues to achieving planning consent are available because of the time and cost implications.

Project Programme

Timetables for appeals procedures

The target timetables for appeals have been set out by PINS following a review of its procedures (it should be noted that actual times are frequently in excess of these and PINS also publish performance data for the previous year which can be more accurate):

- 80% of written representations appeals will be decided within 14 weeks of the start date
- hearing events will be fixed to open no later than 10 weeks after the start date, meaning that 80% can be decided within 14 weeks of the start date
- non-bespoke inquiries will be fixed to open no later than 16 weeks after the start date, meaning that 80% can be decided within 22 weeks of the start date.

www.planningportal.gov.uk/uploads/pins/appeals_review_annex_planning_agent.pdf

The PINS guidance suggest that for inquiries that are likely to sit for more than three days the appellant should discuss a draft bespoke timetable with the LPA and other parties. Factors that can influence the ability to meet these targets are the availability of the parties, key witnesses and an inspector with the appropriate expertise as well as a suitable venue, usually the council chamber or committee room. Politically contentious cases, particularly those involving green belt or wind farms, may be called-in by the Secretary of State, which can delay the release of decision notices for many months.

Project Budget

The costs of appealing can result in the overall cost of obtaining planning consent exceeding the amount originally budgeted. The costs will vary depending on the size and nature of the case, but can be required to cover:

| preparing the appeal statement
| commissioning additional expert evidence
| managing the appeal process

I preparing section 106 agreements (which have to be agreed and signed before the appeal is heard)

I attendance at the site visit, hearing or inquiry by the agent and expert witnesses

I legal representation at a public inquiry.

Domestic projects at Stage 3

Appeals

As with the application, householder appeals have a separate application form. Most domestic appeals are heard as written representations. The client will need to be aware of the inspector's site visit, and the protocol preventing representations being made to the inspector while the visit is in progress.

Chapter summary   3

The output from Stage 3 usually contains sufficient definition within the Developed Design to enable a planning application that will represent the final intention of the project without material amendments to the approved scheme.

Making a planning application is more than assembly and submission of the forms, fee, certificates, drawings and other supporting documentation. By tracking the application and volunteering further assistance at key points in the determination period, the chances of the application succeeding are enhanced. The project lead or agent may also be called upon to make a presentation to the planning committee. If the application is refused, the benefits of appealing should be considered. If it is decided to pursue this route, the project lead should set out the implications for the Project Budget and Project Programme for the client and project team.

Technical Design

Chapter overview

It is advisable that work does not commence at Stage 4 until planning permission has been obtained due to the risks associated with obtaining consent. Once permission is obtained the conditions attached to it can be addressed as required. Pre-commencement conditions must be approved by the planning authority before work on site begins at Stage 5 and in accordance with the Design Programme. This chapter describes the requirements for conditions and how, if necessary, they can be challenged. The provision of detailed information to the planning authority will be part of the Technical Design and the responsibility of the relevant design team member identified in the Design Responsibility Matrix or Schedules of Services.

The key coverage in this chapter is as follows:

Interpreting the decision notice

Conditions and their implications

Challenging conditions

Making applications for amendments

Making applications for listed building consent

Introduction

Previous chapters have demonstrated the risks associated with obtaining planning permission and it is advisable to secure consent before engaging the design team in the Technical Design stage. However, the planning process is a long one and some clients will balance the risk of refusal against the costs of delay and instruct work to commence at Stage 4, while the application is being processed. In doing so the client should confirm that they have considered the risks and any changes to Stage 4 information that result from the planning negotiations will be instructed via the Change Control Procedures.

During the application process it should be possible to discuss the conditions that the planning officers are recommending to be attached to the approval so that, unless the elected members have asked for modification or imposition of additional conditions, the design team will be prepared for them.

This chapter discusses the types of conditions, how they should be met and when they should be discharged. Conditions should meet the 'six tests'; if they do not, and they are detrimental to the scheme and the client's requirements, they can be challenged at appeal.

Applications for listed building consent usually require a considerable amount of technical detail and require much of the Stage 4 work to be completed before they are submitted. The fee profile for the work should recognise this level of input early on in the project.

What are the Core Objectives of this stage?

The Core Objectives of the RIBA Plan of Work 2013 at Stage 4 are:

4

Technical Design

Tasks ▼

Core Objectives

Prepare **Technical Design** in accordance with **Design Responsibility Matrix** and **Project Strategies** to include all architectural, structural and building services information, specialist subcontractor design and specifications, in accordance with **Design Programme**.

The Technical Design will include the information required to release the pre-commencement conditions and the implications of other technical conditions that may need to be discharged before or during the construction period.

Interpreting the decision notice

Once the planning officers, the planning committee, the inspector or the Secretary of State have decided the application or appeal, the decision notice will be issued. The content of approvals from local planning authorities (LPAs) should not be a surprise to the architect or agent if they have had good communication with the officers throughout the application process and have seen the officers' report to the committee. They may have attended the planning meeting in order to speak and so may have heard of any amendments requested by the members at first hand.

The decision notice is usually sent to the agent submitting the application. It should contain the following:

I Date of consent: the consent is valid from the date it was issued, not from the date of any committee decision
I Description of the proposed development
I The drawings and documents that have been approved: these can be listed as a condition
I Reasons for approval or refusal
I Development plan policies and other policies which are material that have been relied upon
I Conditions
I Reasons for condition
I 'Informatives': the authority may attach guidance on other regulations that must be complied with and details of how to appeal.

Conditions and their implications

Conditions require further action or information from the applicant.

Advice on conditions

Detailed advice on conditions is contained in the Planning Practice Guidance which supports the National Planning Policy Framework. It is available on the Planning Portal at:

http://planningguidance.planningportal.gov.uk/

Conditions are frequently used to require additional details about the scheme or the order that work must be undertaken, usually to ensure safe working conditions or to determine the use of the development. There are many examples of conditions that are too onerous or incorrectly worded or applied, so a good understanding of the requirements of the legislation is advisable for architects and agents. This will ensure they can serve their clients' best interests during the design and construction process and when a scheme is in use. In an appeal situation, it is worth bringing the issue to the attention of the inspector, who will be careful to adhere to the six tests in drafting the conditions, if the appeal is upheld.

Suggested Order for Planning Conditions on a Decision Notice

The Planning Practice Guidance suggests that there should be a clear order to any conditions listed in a decision notice:

1. the standard time limit condition for commencement of development
2. the details and drawings subject to which the planning permission is granted
3. any pre-commencement conditions
4. any pre-occupancy or other stage conditions
5. any conditions relating to post-occupancy monitoring and management.

Time limits

The standard time limits in which development has to commence are set out in the Town and Country Planning Act 1990 as:

- 3 years in which to commence works for full consent
- 3 years for submission of reserved matters if outline consent is granted
- 2 years in which to commence works after approval of reserved matters.

These time limits are deemed to apply even if it is not conditioned. However, the local authority can vary them by reducing the time if an earlier start is required or extending it if the lead-in time for a major project is likely to take more than three years.

Commencement

If the pre-commencement conditions are discharged and a start is made on the building work that is reasonably substantial, such as excavating for and pouring the foundations of a building, then it is deemed that the work has commenced and the permission is then running. The work required to commence a scheme is defined by case law. There is usually then no limit on the time that can be taken to complete the project. This prevents the need for applying for a renewal of an approval at the end of the time limit.

Details and drawings

If the approval sets out what information has been approved it should not be necessary to resubmit that information to satisfy a condition – see the 'six tests' (page 130).

Pre-commencement conditions

These should require only that which it is necessary to be completed before work begins on site. These are known as 'conditions precedent' and can be challenged if found not to meet legal and policy tests. However, if the imposed conditions are lawful then to commence work without complying with them would be unlawful and may be enforced against.

Challenging pre-commencement conditions

LPAs frequently require information not strictly necessary before works commence but there is usually little mileage to be gained in challenging such conditions. Indeed it is helpful to the project to discharge conditions during Stage 4 so that the Technical Design can be completed before construction.

Pre-commencement conditions can require technical design information, such as results of further tests and details of mitigation work for factors such as contaminated land and noise, drainage details and landscape works. This will be provided by different members of the design team and coordinated by the project lead. Occasionally, despite careful consultation, the additional work required to release conditions will not have been predicted at the time that the design team and specialist consultants are appointed and the additional work will need to be instructed by the client.

'Grampian' conditions

Named after the case of *Grampian Regional Council* v *City of Aberdeen District Council* [1984], these are negative conditions that prevent the development or its occupancy until works outside the application site have been undertaken. Typically, these are highway improvements. Such a condition can only be considered valid if there is a reasonable expectation that the condition would be fulfilled.

Pre-occupancy or other stage conditions

These should be discharged either during construction in Stage 5 if they relate to working practices, or at the end of the construction period at Stage 6 if they relate to actions or information required before occupancy. In certain situations conditions requiring the phasing of work will be imposed.

Post-occupancy monitoring or management

These form part of Stage 7 tasks and can include restrictions on hours of operation.

Challenging conditions

If an applicant is unhappy with a condition or, once the development is operational, decides that they wish to amend a condition, an application can be made to the planning authority to alter or remove the condition on the original approval.

Example of varying a condition

A planning approval for a hot food takeaway restricts the hours of operation to noon to 11pm. The takeaway has been trading for some time when a nightclub opens up nearby and the owner wishes to take advantage of the potential late night trade. The applicant applies for a variation on the condition to extend the opening hours to 3am.

Example of removing a condition

A rural house has a condition restricting occupancy to those engaged in agriculture and their dependants, known as an agricultural tie. A potential purchaser who is not engaged in agriculture wishes to remove the condition and occupy the house. The applicant establishes that the house could not be sold with the tie in place as there is no need for rural worker housing in the area and applies to have the condition removed, providing the evidence of the lack of need.

If the application is refused, the applicant can appeal within six months of the decision letter being issued.

If a condition does not meet one or more of the six tests set out overleaf it is possible to appeal to have the condition removed within six months of the decision letter being issued. As appealing can be a lengthy and sometimes expensive procedure, an assessment needs to be made of the impact of the condition on the success of the project: action should be taken only if the expenditure of time and money can be justified.

Paragraph 206 of the National Planning Policy Framework

Planning conditions should only be imposed where they are necessary, relevant to planning and to the development to be permitted, enforceable, precise and reasonable in all other respects.

The Planning Practice Guidance analyses each of these six tests in turn:

Key considerations for the six tests for conditions from the Planning Practice Guidance

Necessary

Will it be appropriate to refuse planning permission without the requirements imposed by the condition?

- A condition must not be imposed unless there is a definite planning reason for it, ie it is needed to make the development acceptable in planning terms.
- If a condition is wider in scope than is necessary to achieve the desired objective it will fail the test of necessity.

Relevant to planning

Does the condition relate to planning objectives and is it within the scope of the permission to which it is to be attached?

- A condition must not be used to control matters that are subject to specific control elsewhere in planning legislation (for example, advertisement control, listed building consents, or tree preservation).
- Specific controls outside planning legislation may provide an alternative means of managing certain matters (for example, works on public highways often require highway authority consent).

Relevant to the development to be permitted

Does the condition fairly and reasonably relate to the development to be permitted?

- It is not sufficient that a condition is related to planning objectives: it must also be justified by the nature or impact of the development permitted.
- A condition cannot be imposed in order to remedy a pre-existing problem or issue not created by the proposed development.

Enforceable

Would it be practically possible to enforce the condition?

– Unenforceable conditions include those for which it would, in practice, be impossible to detect a contravention or remedy any breach of the condition, or those concerned with matters over which the applicant has no control.

Precise

Is the condition written in a way that makes it clear to the applicant and others what must be done to comply with it?

– Poorly worded conditions do not clearly state what is required and when must not be used.

Reasonable in all other respects

Is the condition reasonable?

– Conditions which place unjustifiable and disproportionate burdens on an applicant will fail the test of reasonableness.
– Unreasonable conditions cannot be used to make development that is unacceptable in planning terms acceptable.

Even small projects can have many conditions attached, which can delay the commencement of construction work. Sometimes it is advisable to supply with the application information that is likely to be required, to avoid a condition being imposed; however, the client may need to wait for approval and with it the ability to secure finance before undertaking investigation work. This was the case in the example below, which had both ground contamination and archaeological investigations required by condition.

Example of conditions on a small housing project

This decision is subject to conditions. These are listed below together with the reasons for imposing each one. These conditions must be fully complied with.

1. The development, hereby permitted, shall be begun not later than three years from the date of this permission.

    Reason: In accordance with the requirements of section 91 of the Town and Country Planning Act, 1990 as amended by section 51 of the Planning and Compulsory Purchase Act 2004.

2. The development hereby permitted shall be carried out in accordance with the following approved plans.

    Reason: For the avoidance of doubt and in order to define the permission.

3. The external facing brickwork shall be in accordance with the samples as provided and as stated on the detailed drawings nos. xyz received 8 January 2013.

    Reason: To ensure the satisfactory completed appearance of the development and for the avoidance of doubt.

4. No development, excluding site works, shall commence until such time as details of the external roofing materials to be used for the development hereby permitted have been agreed in writing by the Local Planning Authority. The work shall be completed in accordance with the agreed details.

    Reason: To ensure the satisfactory completed appearance of the development.

5. No development, including site works, shall begin until a landscaping scheme has been submitted to and agreed in writing by the local planning authority.

    Reason: To make sure that a satisfactory landscaping scheme for the development is agreed.

6. The landscaping scheme shall be fully completed, in accordance with the details agreed under the terms of the above condition, in the first planting and seeding seasons following the first occupation of any part of the development or in accordance with a programme previously agreed in writing by the local planning authority. Any trees or plants removed, dying, being severely damaged or becoming seriously diseased, within five years of planting shall be

replaced in the following planting season by trees or plants of a size and species similar to those originally required to be planted.

Reason: To make sure that the appearance of the completed development is satisfactory and to help assimilate the development into its surroundings.

7. Prior to first occupation of the development hereby approved, all parking and vehicle access areas, shall be hard surfaced in a porous material, where practicable, and drained in accordance with a scheme to be first submitted to, and approved in writing by, the Local Planning Authority. The approved scheme shall be retained for such purposes in perpetuity.

    Reason: In the interests of visual amenity in the locality; the safety of users of the adjoining highway, and to reduce the risk of flooding in accordance with guidance in the National Planning Policy Framework 2012.

8. The integral garages to the dwelling houses hereby approved shall be retained for the parking of vehicles and at no time shall be converted into ancillary residential accommodation without the prior consent of the local planning authority.

    Reason: In order that adequate off street car parking is retained; in the interests of vehicular and pedestrian safety on the adjoining highway.

9. Prior to commencement of the development hereby approved, excluding site works, drainage details for the disposal of surface water, incorporating sustainable drainage principles, where practicable, shall be submitted to, and approved in writing by, the Local Planning Authority and implemented in accordance with the approved details prior to the development being completed and occupied.

    Reason: To ensure the development is provided with a satisfactory means of drainage as well as to reduce the risk of flooding in accordance with guidance in the National Planning Policy Framework 2012.

10. Unless otherwise agreed by the Local Planning Authority, no development shall take place until a site investigation of the nature and extent of contamination has been carried out in accordance with a methodology which has previously been submitted to and approved in writing by the Local Planning Authority. The results of the site investigation shall be made available to the local planning authority before any

Example of conditions on a small housing project (*continued*)

development begins. If any contamination is found during the site investigation, a report specifying the measures to be taken to remediate the site to render it suitable for the development hereby permitted shall be submitted to and approved in writing by the local planning authority. The site shall be remediated in accordance with the approved measures before development begins. If, during the course of development, any contamination is found which has not been identified in the site investigation, additional measures for the remediation of this source of contamination shall be submitted to and approved in writing by the local planning authority. The remediation of the site shall incorporate the approved additional measures.

Reason: To prevent unacceptable risks to health and pollution of the environment in accordance with the aims and objectives of the National Planning Policy Framework. Where a site is affected by contamination or land stability issues, responsibility for securing a safe development rests with the developer and/or landowner.

11. All building work and any other construction related activities shall only take place between the hours of 0800 and 1800 on Mondays to Saturdays with no work taking place at all on Sundays and Bank Holidays.

    Reason: In order to protect the amenity of nearby residential occupiers.

12. No development shall commence until a programme of archaeological work, including a Written Scheme of Investigation, has been submitted to and approved in writing by the Local Planning Authority.

    Reason: In the interests of identifying, investigating and recording features of archaeological interest.

13. Development of any phase of the works shall only take place in accordance with the Written Scheme of Investigation, as approved by the above Condition. Any part of the development shall not thereafter be brought into use until the site investigation and post investigation report has been completed for that element, in accordance with the programme set out in the approved Written Scheme of Investigation.

    Reason: In the interests of identifying, investigating and recording features of archaeological interest.

Conditions tracker

| Condition type | Condition no | Planning timetable | | | | Outputs | | | | | Project implications | | |
		Due by	Date submitted	LPA target determination date	Date approved	Drawings	Testing	Reports	Operations	Schedule of Services	Budget	Programme	Construction Strategy
Time limit	1											start date	
Approved drawings	2	site start				as amended							start date	
Pre-commencement	3	site start				as amended							start date	
		site start				as amended							start date	
Grampian													phasing?	
Construction stage														
		handover											phasing?	
Pre-occupancy		handover												
		handover												
Post-occupancy														

Making applications for amendments

Amendments to the design made during the Technical Design stage may change the scheme that has been granted planning approval. These can arise due to:

I   design changes instructed by the client
I   technical revisions from the design team as the scheme is developed
I   value engineering
I   changes in availability of materials and components.

Applications should be made for material or non-material amendments (see page 144: Stage 5) as soon as the changes are identified. It is advisable to obtain approval from the planning authority before the changes are put through the Change Control Procedures and instructed to prevent any delay to the project. The project team should be made aware of the consequences for planning of any change.

Making applications for listed buildings consent

Listed building and conservation area consents are covered by different legislation; however, as the work frequently involves operational development, planning permission may also be required. The level of detail needed to support the application is usually greater than Stage 3 outputs and can include full-size details and specifications of craft techniques. This should be taken into account in preparing the fee profile and Design Programme for these works. The subsequent approval period needs to be factored into the Project Programme and may impact on the proposed date for work to start on site.

Domestic projects at Stage 4

Once planning permission has been obtained and the decision
notice issued, the conditions attached to the permission
should be discussed with the client and arrangements made
to discharge them. When clients intend to take on the project
themselves from Stage 4 they should be advised that they need
to apply for consent for pre-commencement conditions and that
they must get these approved before any work commences. They
may possibly require assistance in identifying suitably qualified
professionals for additional technical support. Clients should
also be advised of the implications of making changes to the
approved scheme.

Chapter summary   4

Obtaining planning permission for a project is a major milestone.
However, it is important to take into account the additional work
that will be required to put the approved scheme into operation.
Discharging the conditions imposed can require further site
investigations and additional detailed design work and the Project
Programme and the Project Budget should account for this. If
conditions are imposed that threaten the viability of the scheme, the
planning strategy may have to be amended to include an application
to alter or remove a condition or an appeal to have the condition
removed.

Stage 5

Construction

Chapter overview

Once the pre-commencement conditions have been discharged and work has commenced, the planning permission is implemented. However, there remains a responsibility to comply with construction stage conditions and to release others. The project has to be constructed in accordance with the approved drawings and documents; therefore, if any changes are made that affect planning, additional consent will be required. Change Control Procedures should identify the implications for the Project Programme and Project Budget of obtaining approval for material and non-material amendments to the planning approval.

The key coverage in this chapter is as follows:

Determining responsibility for release of conditions during construction

Determining responsibility for compliance with conditions during construction

Identifying the planning implications of changes made during construction

Providing planning drawings and documentation for the 'As-constructed' Information

Introduction

This chapter covers managing the planning consent during construction, identifying responsibilities for releasing conditions and complying with others that govern how the work is to be carried out. The project lead has to be aware that any amendments made to the scheme that affect the approved scheme will have to be approved by the planning authority and applications made for material and non-material amendments. This additional planning process carries the risk of delay to the Project Programme while consent is sought or, if ignored, risk of enforcement action. The 'As-constructed' Information should include a complete set of drawing as amended and approved and all relevant decision notices.

What are the Core Objectives of this stage?

The Core Objectives of the RIBA Plan of Work 2013 at Stage 5 are:

5

Construction

Tasks ▼

Core
Objectives

Offsite manufacturing and onsite **Construction** in accordance with **Construction Programme** and resolution of **Design Queries** from site as they arise.

The planning process can impact on the Construction Programme if there are delays in releasing conditions or if applications for non-material amendments or revised full applications have to be made as the result of changes to the approved scheme.

Determining responsibility for release of conditions during construction

The project lead will need to ensure that the Building Contract and any other contract documents make it clear who is responsible for compiling supporting documentation and making applications for the release of those conditions that remain to be released once the construction stage has commenced. Such conditions can include the reports of watching briefs during excavation for archaeology and outstanding approvals of materials. At this stage, in some forms of procurement, the contractor will be given responsibility for discharge of conditions. In traditional contracts, the lead designer will make the applications for release of conditions on behalf of the client.

Determining responsibility for compliance with conditions during construction

If the planning consent carries conditions that determine how the work shall be carried out, these must form part of the Building Contract and the contractor is required to include them in the Construction Strategy and adhere to them. Such conditions may typically:

I   require work to be carried out in accordance with an agreed phasing sequence
I   limit the hours of construction
I   limit the times or method of delivery of materials to site
I   require the control of dust and/or noise levels.

Identifying the planning implications of changes made during construction

However carefully buildings are designed and however accurate the Stage 3 outputs used for the planning application are, there will usually be some subsequent amendments to the project that are material to planning and that will require an additional consent. These can arise for a number of reasons, including:

I   design changes instructed by the client
I   technical revisions in response to site conditions

I value engineering
I changes in availability of materials and components.

Without planning approval for the amendment, construction work can only continue up until the point that the change is to be implemented. There is, therefore, the potential for delay to the Project Programme, and the associated costs that can arise, if there is insufficient notice of the need for an amendment, the application for the amendment is delayed or the decision process is prolonged. If work proceeds without the consent in place there is a danger of enforcement action (see page 160: Stage 7).

There are three types of amendment: material, minor material and non-material. The nature of the amendment and the appropriate route to approval are determined by the local authority on a case-by-case basis, and as each carries the risk of delay, or even refusal, assessment of the risks to the project should be made as soon as a change is identified.

Material amendments

Where the amendments are fundamental or substantial, a new planning application will be necessary.

Minor material amendment

The Planning Practice Guidance definition of minor material amendment

There is no statutory definition of a 'minor material amendment' but it is likely to include any amendment where its scale and/ or nature results in a development which is not substantially different from the one which has been approved. Pre-application discussions will be useful to judge the appropriateness of this route in advance of an application being submitted.

The determination period for a minor material amendment is eight or 13 weeks, as for a planning application, but the result will be a new approval with the same expiry date as the original approval. There is a right to appeal. Typically, the inclusion of additional windows or a change of materials would be considered a minor material amendment, but it is important to negotiate this with the planning authority on a case-by-case basis.

Non-material amendment

The Planning Practice Guidance definition of non-material amendment

There is no statutory definition of 'non-material'. This is because it will be dependent on the context of the overall scheme – an amendment that is non-material in one context may be material in another. The local planning authority must be satisfied that the amendment sought is non-material in order to grant an application under section 96A of the Town and Country Planning Act 1990.

The determination period for a non-material amendment is 28 days, or longer if previously agreed in writing. The result is not a new approval and there is no right to appeal.

The Planning Practice Guidance sets out the requirements for each type of amendment.

Providing planning drawings and documentation for the 'As-constructed' Information

A key output of Stage 5 is the 'As-constructed' Information, which includes the latest release of drawings for construction. These will include any amendments granted consent and should be accompanied by the decision notices relating to each approval for the client's records. If the building is sold in the future, evidence of all approvals will be required as part of the conveyance and the client should be advised of this.

Domestic projects at Stage 5

Clients should be advised of any conditions that regulate the work on site and these should be incorporated into the preliminaries of the construction contract. The client should be advised that any changes to the scheme that are material to planning will require further planning consents and will therefore risk delaying the project.

Chapter summary · 5

In order to secure and maintain full planning consent for the project, the project team must be aware of the need to obtain approvals for any outstanding conditions or amendments and that the time required to secure these can affect the Project Programme.

The completed project should have been constructed in accordance with any construction stage conditions and in accordance with the approved drawings, including any approved amendments. Any amendments should be recorded on the 'As-constructed' Information completed at the end of Stage 5.

Handover and Close Out

Chapter overview

There are few actions required with respect to planning at this stage, with the exception of ensuring that any pre-occupancy conditions are complied with.

The key coverage in this chapter is as follows:

Complying with pre-occupancy conditions

Introduction

This chapter covers the requirement to discharge any pre-occupancy conditions.

What are the Core Objectives of this stage?

The Core Objectives of the RIBA Plan of Work 2013 at Stage 6 are:

Tasks ▼	**6** Handover and Close Out
Core Objectives	Handover of building and conclusion of **Building Contract**.

Planning issues at this stage are generally restricted to the discharge of pre-occupancy conditions.

Complying with pre-occupancy conditions

The planning consent may have imposed conditions that must be complied with before the building can be occupied. These can include:

I submission of details that were not necessary before commencement of work, eg submission for approval of a landscape scheme that will be implemented in the planting season following completion of the building

I conditions that require that the performance of the building meets a set standard, eg sound insulation or environmental performance

I requirements to make the building or access safe before occupancy, such as ensuring that access and parking are in place.

The project lead should ensure that these conditions have been complied with and that the necessary approvals have been obtained. The client should be informed of these requirements and advised of any potential delay to occupying the building.

Domestic projects at Stage 6

Minor transgressions of planning law may be overlooked by the planning authority at the time, but it is important that the householder regularises all development work. When the householder comes to sell the house at a later date, any irregularities will be picked up by conveyancing solicitors as a risk of enforcement against future owners of the property.

Chapter summary 6

The project lead should ensure that pre-occupancy conditions are complied with.

Stage 7

In Use

Chapter overview

At this stage the responsibility for the project and its use have passed to the client. However, there may be conditions determining how the building can be used and advice on these will need to be provided. As part of the project review there should be consideration of the effectiveness of the planning strategy and its delivery. If planning matters have not been complied with, advice on the procedures surrounding planning enforcement may be required.

The key coverage in this chapter is as follows:

Complying with 'in-use' conditions

Reviewing the implementation of the planning strategy and implications for further development

Advising the client on planning enforcement

Introduction

This chapter covers compliance with any in-use conditions that may have been imposed on the planning consent, reviewing the success of the planning strategy in the Post-occupancy Evaluation and reviewing the Project Performance, which are carried out at this stage

Also included is an overview of planning enforcement, as it may become necessary to assist clients who are faced with enforcement action. This is not part of the usual Schedule of Services within the RIBA Plan of Work 2013, but it may become an additional service as a consequence of non-compliance and when planning law has been breached. Enforcement is covered at this stage as this is when any action is most likely to occur.

What are the Core Objectives of this stage?

The Core Objectives of the RIBA Plan of Work 2013 at Stage 7 are:

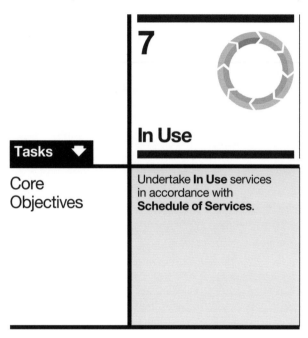

7	
	In Use
Tasks ▼	
Core Objectives	Undertake **In Use** services in accordance with **Schedule of Services**.

Planning issues at this stage are generally restricted to compliance with in-use conditions; however, any unresolved planning matters may result in enforcement action by the planning authority.

Complying with in-use conditions

Planning approvals may contain conditions that require post-occupancy control or management of how the development is used. Conditions can include limitations on:

I opening hours
I sound levels or other possible types of nuisance
I months of occupancy (usually for holiday accommodation)
I type or maximum percentage of a building that can be given to a particular use class.

These fall outside the responsibility of the project team, but the client needs to be briefed on their implications and how to demonstrate ongoing compliance to the planning authority, such as keeping records of occupancy, if this is part of the condition.

Advice can be provided on making applications to remove conditions that restrict the effective use of the development or on appealing these conditions if within the timeframe for appeal after the consent has been granted (see page 128: Stage 4).

Reviewing the implementation of the planning strategy and implications for further development

The Post-occupancy Evaluation determines whether the Project Outcomes set out in the Final Project Brief have been achieved. The Final Project Brief is issued at the end of Stage 3 and will have included the planning consent and its implications for the Project Programme and Project Budget, including the discharge of any conditions. The review is likely to include the implications of any changes made after Stage 3 and the consequent actions required to maintain the planning consent for the project.

In addition there should be a review of the Project Performance, which includes the performance of the project team. The decisions taken in devising and implementing the planning strategy can be reviewed and, if the project is part of ongoing development, the future approach to planning can be revised in the light of the experience gained in the completed and occupied building or buildings. The review can also inform the approach taken on new projects.

Project review – planning considerations

The project review can include consideration of the effectiveness and desirability of:

– early engagement with policymaking
– the use of outline applications
– matters to be reserved
– conduct of pre-application discussions
– the use of design review
– effectiveness of members of the consultant team (design team)
– the use of planning performance agreements
– approaches to community liaison
– the presentation of applications
– control over unforeseen amendments.

Advising the client on planning enforcement

If the development or the use of land or buildings is carried out without or in contravention of a planning approval (a breach of planning law), the local planning authority (LPA) can enforce. There are a number of options available to the LPA, which are set out in the Planning Practice Guidance under Ensuring Effective Enforcement and can be summarised as follows:

I No formal action.
I Retrospective planning application: there is only one opportunity to gain retrospective approval and it may be advisable to link this to an appeal.
I Planning Contravention Notice: used to obtain information about the breach, which may or may not lead to:
  o Enforcement Notice: sets out what the breach is and how it is to be remedied. There is a right to appeal (see below).
  o Planning Enforcement Order: enforced by the magistrates courts, this is used where there has been a deliberate attempt to conceal a major breach.
  o Stop Notice: used with an enforcement notice to require operations or use to cease. Only used for actions that threaten public safety or amenity or to prevent serious or irreversible harm to the environment in the surrounding area.
  o Temporary Stop Notice: can be issued before an enforcement notice and lasts for 28 days.

○ Breach of Condition Notice: alternative to an enforcement notice for breach of conditions.
○ Injunction: the most serious enforcement action, which can result in imprisonment if not complied with.

Enforcement action is underpinned by the courts and failure to comply can result in fines and, in the case of an injunction, imprisonment.

The first notification is usually receipt of the Planning Contravention Notice. The owner should seek specialist planning and legal advice and decide whether to comply with the enforcement notice, if it is forthcoming, or appeal.

Enforcement appeals

Guidance on the grounds for appeal

Advice on the seven grounds for appeal can be found on the Planning Portal at:

www.planningportal.gov.uk/uploads/pins/procedural_guidance_enforcement_appeals.pdf

The grounds for appeal can be summarised as:

I Ground (a): that planning permission should be granted for what is alleged in the notice (or that the condition or limitation referred to in the enforcement notice should be removed).
I Ground (b): that the breach of control alleged in the enforcement notice has not occurred as a matter of fact.
I Ground (c): that there has not been a breach of planning control.
I Ground (d): that at the time the enforcement notice was issued it was too late to take enforcement action against the matters stated in the notice.
I Ground (e): that the notice was not properly served on everyone with an interest in the land.
I Ground (f): steps required to comply with the requirements of the enforcement notice are excessive and lesser steps would overcome the objections.
I Ground (g): that the time given to comply with the notice is too short.

Ground (a) requires documentation to support a retrospective planning application and a planning fee. The other grounds require evidence to support the appeal. Enforcement appeals frequently combine a number of the grounds, so that if one fails there is a fallback position.

Chapter summary 7

The in-use conditions are the responsibility of the client, who will need the advice of the project lead on how to comply with them.

Effective review of both the outcomes of the project and the performance of the project team will inform future projects and can lead to future successful outcomes.

Although not part of the RIBA Plan of Work 2013 services, professional assistance to overcome planning enforcement can be valuable for clients when there is a failure to deliver a project within planning law. Best practice will ensure that enforcement is avoided, but if clients wish to take risks with the planning system, the project lead must be in a position to advise them of the consequences. This is a specialist area of planning practice and expert advice may be required.

Further reading

Online

RIBA Plan of Work 2013: ribaplanofwork.com/
Essential resource for the context of this book.

The Planning Portal: planningportal.gov.uk/
For forms, information and online tools and links to government policy.

National Planning Policy Framework: gov.uk/government/publications/
national-planning-policy-framework--2
Introduced In March 2012, the National Planning Policy Framework
reduced over 1,000 pages of national policy to around 50. It abolished
the National Planning Policy Statements and the earlier National
Planning Policy Guidance notes.

Planning Practice Guidance: http://planningguidance.planningportal.
gov.uk/
Accessed through the Planning Portal, the online guidance is updated
as required. Users can sign up for email alerts to changes. The site
uses a menu-based navigation system through many pages of FAQ-
style topics listed under 42 categories.

The Planning Advisory Service: www.pas.gov.uk/
Advice for planning authorities; useful as a source of information, but
it does not answer queries from private practitioners or the general
public.

Planning Aid: rtpi.org.uk/planning-aid/
Provides planning support to individuals and neighbourhood plans,
but not to professionals.

GOV.UK: gov.uk/
Provides information on other legislation.

English Heritage: english-heritage.org.uk/professional/advice/our-planning-role/
Provides background to its role in the historic environment; see particularly http://list.english-heritage.org.uk/mapsearch.aspx, which provides excellent maps locating heritage assets.

Environment Agency: apps.environment-agency.gov.uk/wiyby/37837. aspx
For flood maps and contaminated land.

Magic Maps: magic.gov.uk/
Useful interactive mapping tool for natural and historic environment. Hints for successful use: be selective about the information to be shown as it can become overloaded, and zoom out to capture the green belt layer, which does not work at small scale.

RTPI Good Practice Guides including:
rtpi.org.uk/media/6312/Good-Practice-Guide-to-Public-Engagement-in-Development-Scheme-High-Res.pdf
A colourful guide to public engagement produced by Planning Aid.

RTPI The Handy Guide to Planning 2012
http://www.rtpi.org.uk/media/1454776/planning_handy_guide_2012_5_final.pdf
A basic overview of the planning system.

RIBA Guide to Localism: Opportunities for Architects
Part one: Neighbourhood Planning
Part two: Getting Community Engagement Right
www.architecture.com
Excellent practical advice and sources of additional guidance.

Books

Guide to Using the RIBA Plan of Work 2013
Dale Sinclair, May 2013, RIBA Publishing, ISBN: 9781859465042
Framework for this Guide.

RIBA Job Book (9th edition)
Nigel Ostime, May 2013, RIBA Publishing, ISBN: 9781859464960
A practice essential that has been updated to the RIBA Plan of Work 2013.

Assembling a Collaborative Project Team: Practical Tools Including Multidisciplinary Schedules of Services
Dale Sinclair, October 2013, RIBA Publishing, ISBN 9781859464977
Guidance for putting the consultants involved in planning into the project team.

RIBA Plan of Work 2013 Guides:
I *Design Management*
Dale Sinclair, RIBA Publishing, ISBN: 9781859465509
I *Project Leadership*
Nick Willars RIBA Publishing ISBN: 9781859465516
I *Contract Administration*
Ian Davies, RIBA Publishing, ISBN: 9781859465523

Good Practice Guide: Building Conditions Surveys
Mike Hoxley, July 2009, RIBA Publishing, ISBN: 9781859463086
Advice on surveying buildings as part of Site Information.

Telling & Duxbury's Planning Law and Procedure
Robert Duxbury, December 2012, Oxford University Press
ISBN: 9780199655021
The standard planning law text.

Encyclopedia of Planning Law and Practice, Thompson
The Local Government Library, Sweet and Maxwell
ISBN: 97801421007406
Looseleaf resource running to nine volumes and an index, updated by subscription.

Town planning glossary

Agricultural holdings certificate

All planning applications must be accompanied by an agricultural holdings certificate confirming whether or not any of the land to which the application relates is, or is part of, an agricultural holding.

Area of Outstanding Natural Beauty (AONB)

Nationally designated areas of exceptional landscape character that have a greater level of protection against harmful development.

Areas of constraint

Areas recognised as having exceptional merit for natural or heritage reasons or needed to check the spread of development that are designated for a higher level of protection. See also *Special area designations.*

Article 4 directions

Article 4 directions are put in place by planning authorities to withdraw the automatic approval under permitted development (PD) rights to some or all of the PD rights in an area.

Betterment

The reduction in the potential impact of a development over the existing use.

Breach of Condition Notice

Issued by a planning authority as an alternative to an enforcement notice for breach of conditions.

Certificate of lawfulness of existing use or development (CLEUD)

CLEUDs establish the lawfulness of an existing use or development that does not have planning consent. It does not grant consent but certifies that the use or development has been in existence long enough to no longer require consent.

Community Infrastructure Levy

The Community Infrastructure Levy can be charged by local authorities on new development. The charges are based on the size and type of the new development. The money can be used to support development by funding local infrastructure.

Delegated powers

Powers granted to senior planning officers to grant consent for minor applications and applications within policy subject to the authority's standing orders.

Design and access statement

A design and access statement (DAS) is a short report accompanying and supporting a planning application for major development. It sets out how a proposed development is a suitable response to the site and its setting, and demonstrates that it can be adequately accessed by prospective users.

Determination period

The time defined as the target period for planning authorities to reach and publish a decision on a planning application.

Development plan

The development plan consists of a number of documents that set out the aspirations for future development in the local area. These include core strategies, local development frameworks and neighbourhood plans and are expressed in written policy and policy maps.

Enabling development

Consents are given for projects that release resources for wider benefit.

Enforcement Notice

Sets out what breach of planning law has occurred and how it is to be remedied.

Grampian conditions

Negative conditions that prevent the development or its occupancy until works outside the application site have been undertaken.

Green belt

Areas of constraint against development around major urban conurbations. The aim of green belt policy is to prevent urban sprawl by keeping land permanently open. Openness is defined as the absence of development.

Heritage asset

A building, monument, site, place, area or landscape identified as having a degree of significance meriting consideration in planning decisions.

Historic environment

The context in which heritage assets are experienced.

Informatives

Guidance on other regulations that must be complied with and details of how to appeal attached by the planning authority to planning decision notices.

Injunction

The most serious enforcement action that can be put in place by the courts. It can result in imprisonment if not complied with.

Lawful development certificate

Issued by planning authorities to confirm that an existing development or a proposal does not require planning permission.

Local Development Order

Local Development Orders can be put into place by a local authority extending permitted development rights usually in order to stimulate economic growth.

Material amendment

An amendment to the approved scheme which is fundamental or substantial and which requires a new planning application.

Material consideration

Material considerations are matters relevant to planning that can be used to justify approval of an application where it goes against policies in the development plan. As they can be negative as well as positive they can also be weighed against the benefits of a proposal.

Minor material amendment

Any amendment where its scale and/ or nature results in a development which is not substantially different from the one which has been approved. This is subject to agreement with the planning authority.

National Planning Policy Framework

In March 2012 the Department for Communities and Local Government introduced the National Planning Policy Framework which reduced over 1,000 pages of national policy to around 50. It abolished the National Planning Policy Statements and the earlier National Planning Policy Guidance notes.

Neighbour consultation scheme

The temporary increase in the permitted size of rear extensions is subject to a scheme by which neighbours are consulted by the planning authority and if no objections are received and the scheme is judged to be acceptable in terms of residential amenity the development is deemed to be approved.

Neighbourhood Development Order

Communities can use neighbourhood planning to permit development in full or in outline – without the need for planning applications. These are called 'Neighbourhood Development Orders'. These do not take effect unless there is a majority of support in a referendum of the neighbourhood.

Neighbourhood plans

These are produced by local communities to add detail to the local plan and represent the community's aspirations for development in their area. They have to be broadly in line with the Local Plan or the emerging plan and to have undertaken a process of public examination and a local referendum before they are adopted.

Non-material amendment

An amendment considered to be neither fundamental nor substantial by the planning authority and which can be determined by an application under section 96A of the Town and Country Planning Act 1990.

Outline application

An outline application reserves matters to be approved in a subsequent reserved matters application.

Ownership certificate

All planning applications must be accompanied by a correctly completed section 12 certificate. The land ownership and interests are identified and if the application area defined by the red line on the plan is not entirely within the ownership and control of the applicant, notices must be served on the other parties.

Permitted development

These are classes of development for which a grant of planning permission is automatically given by national legislation, provided that no restrictive condition is attached or that the development is exempt.

Planning Contravention Notice

A notice to the owner of land used to obtain information about the breach which may or may not lead to an Enforcement Notice.

Planning Enforcement Order

An order issued by a planning authority and enforced by the magistrates courts. This is used where there has been a deliberate attempt to conceal a major breach

Planning performance agreements

Planning performance agreements (PPAs) are the framework for a collaborative process between the LPA, developer and their agents and key stakeholders in developing, processing and determining a planning application.

Planning Policy Guidance Notes (PPGs) and Planning Policy Statements (PPSs)

Planning Policy Guidance Notes, and their replacements Planning Policy Statements, were prepared by the government to provide guidance to local authorities and others on planning policy and the operation of the planning system. They were superseded by the National Planning Policy Framework in

2012, with further guidance provided in the Planning Practice Guidance, first published in March 2014.

Planning Practice Guidance

Online and updated guidance issued by the government, first issued in March 2014, underpinning the National Planning Policy Framework (NPPF). It carries the same weight for decision makers as the NPPF.

Pre-commencement conditions

Conditions attached to a planning approval that require work or further information which must be completed before work begins on site. These are also known as 'conditions precedent'.

Presumption in favour of sustainable development

If a development plan is out of date the NPPF states that there is a presumption in favour of development if it is sustainable. Sustainability is defined in terms of economic, social and environmental dimensions.

Prior Approval Notice

Notice supplied to a planning authority that certain development that may be permitted under permitted development rights is being proposed. This is then checked against the requirements of the General Permitted Development Order as amended before approval is granted.

Section 106 agreement

An agreement under section 106 of the Town and Country Planning Act 1990 can be used to make an otherwise unacceptable proposal acceptable to the planning authority.

Special area designations

Areas recognised as having exceptional merit for natural or heritage reasons that are designated for a higher level of protection. See also *Areas of constraint*.

Stop Notice

Used with an Enforcement Notice to require operations or use to cease. Only used for actions that threaten public safety or amenity or to prevent serious or irreversible harm to the environment in the surrounding area.

Sui generis

Certain uses do not fall within any planning use class and are considered 'sui generis', which translated means of its own kind.

Temporary Stop Notice

Issued before an Enforcement Notice and effective for 28 days.

Tree Preservation Order (TPO)

A written order made by a local planning authority that makes it an offence to cut down, top, lop, uproot, wilfully damage or wilfully destroy a tree scheduled by the LPA.

Twin-track

To submit a duplicate application to the planning authority, which gives them the opportunity to determine the application and avoid the cost of an appeal.

Unitary and non-unitary authorities

Unitary authorities combine the county and district or borough roles. For non-unitary authorities, the roles are separate, with the core strategy produced at county level and shared with the local councils, who each produce their own local development framework.

Use classes

Building uses are grouped into use classes which are defined in the General Permitted Development Order (GPDO). Changing use within a use class is permitted development, as are some changes of use between use classes.

Validation requirements

The information required to support a planning application at submission. These are defined by a national list and locally held lists.

RIBA Plan of Work 2013 glossary

A number of new themes and subject matters have been included in the RIBA Plan of Work 2013. The following presents a glossary of all of the capitalised terms that are used throughout the RIBA Plan of Work 2013. Defining certain terms has been necessary to clarify the intent of a term, to provide additional insight into the purpose of certain terms and to ensure consistency in the interpretation of the RIBA Plan of Work 2013.

'As-constructed' Information

Information produced at the end of a project to represent what has been constructed. This will comprise a mixture of 'as-built' information from specialist subcontractors and the 'final construction issue' from design team members. Clients may also wish to undertake 'as-built' surveys using new surveying technologies to bring a further degree of accuracy to this information.

Building Contract

The contract between the client and the contractor for the construction of the project. In some instances, the **Building Contract** may contain design duties for specialist subcontractors and/or design team members. On some projects, more than one Building Contract may be required; for example, one for shell and core works and another for furniture, fitting and equipment aspects.

Building Information Modelling (BIM)

BIM is widely used as the acronym for 'Building Information Modelling', which is commonly defined (using the Construction Project Information Committee (CPIC) definition) as: 'digital representation of physical and functional characteristics of a facility creating a shared knowledge resource for information about it and forming a reliable basis for decisions during its life cycle, from earliest conception to demolition'.

Business Case

The **Business Case** for a project is the rationale behind the initiation of a new building project. It may consist solely of a reasoned argument. It may contain supporting information, financial appraisals or other background information. It should also highlight initial considerations for the **Project Outcomes**. In summary, it is a combination of objective and subjective considerations. The **Business Case** might be prepared in relation to, for example, appraising a number of sites or in relation to assessing a refurbishment against a new build option.

Change Control Procedures

Procedures for controlling changes to the design and construction following the sign-off of the Stage 2 Concept Design and the **Final Project Brief**.

Common Standards

Publicly available standards frequently used to define project and design management processes in relation to the briefing, designing, constructing, maintaining, operating and use of a building.

Communication Strategy

The strategy that sets out when the project team will meet, how they will communicate effectively and the protocols for issuing information between the various parties, both informally and at Information Exchanges.

Construction Programme

The period in the **Project Programme** and the **Building Contract** for the construction of the project, commencing on the site mobilisation date and ending at **Practical Completion**.

Construction Strategy

A strategy that considers specific aspects of the design that may affect the buildability or logistics of constructing a project, or may affect health and safety aspects. The **Construction Strategy** comprises items such as cranage, site access and accommodation locations, reviews of the supply chain and sources of materials, and specific buildability items, such as the choice of frame (steel or concrete) or the installation of larger items of plant. On a smaller project, the strategy may be restricted to the location of site cabins and storage, and the ability to transport materials up an existing staircase.

Contractor's Proposals

Proposals presented by a contractor to the client in response to a tender that includes the **Employer's Requirements**. The **Contractor's Proposals** may match the **Employer's Requirements**, although certain aspects may be varied based on value engineered solutions and additional information may be submitted to clarify what is included in the tender. The **Contractor's Proposals** form an integral component of the **Building Contract** documentation.

Contractual Tree

A diagram that clarifies the contractual relationship between the client and the parties undertaking the roles required on a project.

Cost Information

All of the project costs, including the cost estimate and life cycle costs where required.

Design Programme

A programme setting out the strategic dates in relation to the design process. It is aligned with the **Project Programme** but is strategic in its nature, due to the iterative nature of the design process, particularly in the early stages.

Design Queries

Queries relating to the design arising from the site, typically managed using a contractor's in-house request for information (RFI) or technical query (TQ) process.

Design Responsibility Matrix

A matrix that sets out who is responsible for designing each aspect of the project and when. This document sets out the extent of any performance specified design. The **Design Responsibility Matrix** is created at a strategic level at Stage 1 and fine tuned in response to the Concept Design at the end of Stage 2 in order to ensure that there are no design responsibility ambiguities at Stages 3, 4 and 5.

Employer's Requirements

Proposals prepared by design team members. The level of detail will depend on the stage at which the tender is issued to the contractor. The **Employer's Requirements** may comprise a mixture of prescriptive elements and descriptive elements to allow the contractor a degree of flexibility in determining the **Contractor's Proposals**.

Feasibility Studies

Studies undertaken on a given site to test the feasibility of the **Initial Project Brief** on a specific site or in a specific context and to consider how site-wide issues will be addressed.

Feedback

Feedback from the project team, including the end users, following completion of a building.

Final Project Brief

The **Initial Project Brief** amended so that it is aligned with the Concept Design and any briefing decisions made during Stage 2. (Both the Concept Design and **Initial Project Brief** are Information Exchanges at the end of Stage 2.)

Handover Strategy

The strategy for handing over a building, including the requirements for phased handovers, commissioning, training of staff or other factors crucial to the successful occupation of a building. On some projects, the Building Services Research and Information Association (BSRIA) Soft Landings process is used as the basis for formulating the strategy and undertaking a **Post-occupancy Evaluation** (www.bsria. co.uk/services/design/soft-landings/).

Health and Safety Strategy

The strategy covering all aspects of health and safety on the project, outlining legislative requirements as well as other project initiatives, including the **Maintenance and Operational Strategy**.

Information Exchange

The formal issue of information for review

and sign-off by the client at key stages of the project. The project team may also have additional formal **Information Exchanges** as well as the many informal exchanges that occur during the iterative design process.

Initial Project Brief

The brief prepared following discussions with the client to ascertain the **Project Objectives**, the client's **Business Case** and, in certain instances, in response to site **Feasibility Studies**.

Maintenance and Operational Strategy

The strategy for the maintenance and operation of a building, including details of any specific plant required to replace components.

Post-occupancy Evaluation

Evaluation undertaken post occupancy to determine whether the **Project Outcomes**, both subjective and objective, set out in the **Final Project Brief** have been achieved.

Practical Completion

Practical Completion is a contractual term used in the **Building Contract** to signify the date on which a project is handed over to the client. The date triggers a number of contractual mechanisms.

Project Budget

The client's budget for the project, which may include the construction cost as well as the cost of certain items required post completion and during the project's operational use.

Project Execution Plan

The **Project Execution Plan** is produced in collaboration between the project lead and lead designer, with contributions from other designers and members of the project team. The **Project Execution Plan** sets out the processes and protocols to be used to develop the design. It is sometimes referred to as a project quality plan.

Project Information

Information, including models, documents, specifications, schedules and spreadsheets, issued between parties during each stage and in formal Information Exchanges at the end of each stage.

Project Objectives

The client's key objectives as set out in the **Initial Project Brief**. The document includes, where appropriate, the employer's **Business Case**, **Sustainability Aspirations** or other aspects that may influence the preparation of the brief and, in turn, the Concept Design stage. For example, **Feasibility Studies** may be required in order to test the **Initial Project Brief** against a given site, allowing certain high-level briefing issues to be considered before design work commences in earnest.

Project Outcomes

The desired outcomes for the project (for example, in the case of a hospital this might be a reduction in recovery times). The outcomes may include operational aspects and a mixture of subjective and objective criteria.

Project Performance

The performance of the project, determined using **Feedback**, including about the performance of the project team and the performance of the building against the desired **Project Outcomes**.

Project Programme

The overall period for the briefing, design, construction and post-completion activities of a project.

Project Roles Table

A table that sets out the roles required on a project as well as defining the stages during which those roles are required and the parties responsible for carrying out the roles.

Project Strategies

The strategies developed in parallel with the Concept Design to support the design and, in certain instances, to respond to the **Final Project Brief** as it is concluded. These strategies typically include:

I   acoustic strategy
I   fire engineering strategy
I   **Maintenance and Operational Strategy**
I   **Sustainability Strategy**
I   building control strategy
I   **Technology Strategy.**

These strategies are usually prepared in outline at Stage 2 and in detail at Stage 3, with the recommendations absorbed into the Stage 4 outputs and Information Exchanges.

The strategies are not typically used for construction purposes because they may contain recommendations or information that contradict the drawn information. The intention is that they should be transferred into the various models or drawn information.

Quality Objectives

The objectives that set out the quality aspects of a project. The objectives may comprise both subjective and objective aspects, although subjective aspects may be subject to a design quality indicator (DQI) benchmark review during the **Feedback** period.

Research and Development

Project-specific research and development responding to the **Initial Project Brief** or in response to the Concept Design as it is developed.

Risk Assessment

The **Risk Assessment** considers the various design and other risks on a project and how each risk will be managed and the party responsible for managing each risk.

Schedule of Services

A list of specific services and tasks to be undertaken by a party involved in the project which is incorporated into their professional services contract.

Site Information

Specific **Project Information** in the form of specialist surveys or reports relating to the project- or site-specific context.

Strategic Brief

The brief prepared to enable the Strategic Definition of the project. Strategic considerations might include considering different sites, whether to extend, refurbish or build new and the key **Project Outcomes** as well as initial considerations for the **Project Programme** and assembling the project team.

Sustainability Aspirations

The client's aspirations for sustainability, which may include additional objectives, measures or specific levels of performance in relation to international standards, as well as details of specific demands in relation to operational or facilities management issues.

The **Sustainability Strategy** will be prepared in response to the **Sustainability Aspirations** and will include specific additional items, such as an energy plan and ecology plan and the design life of the building, as appropriate.

Sustainability Strategy

The strategy for delivering the **Sustainability Aspirations**.

Technology Strategy

The strategy established at the outset of a project that sets out technologies, including Building Information Modelling (BIM) and any supporting processes, and the specific software packages that each member of the project team will use. Any interoperability issues can then be addressed before the design phases commence.

This strategy also considers how information is to be communicated (by email, file transfer protocol (FTP) site or using a managed third party common data environment) as well as the file formats in which information will provided. The **Project Execution Plan** records agreements made.

Work in Progress

Work in Progress is ongoing design work that is issued between designers to facilitate the iterative coordination of each designer's output. Work issued as **Work in Progress** is signed off by the internal design processes of each designer and is checked and coordinated by the lead designer.

Index

Note: page numbers in italics refer to figures; page numbers in bold refer to tables.